Branding TV
Principles and Practices

Branding TV

Principles and Practices

By

Walter McDowell, Ph.D.
and
Alan Batten

ELSEVIER

AMSTERDAM • BOSTON • HEIDELBERG • LONDON
NEW YORK • OXFORD • PARIS • SAN DIEGO
SAN FRANCISCO • SINGAPORE • SYDNEY • TOKYO

Focal Press is an imprint of Elsevier

Focal
Press

Acquisitions Editor: Angelina Ward
Project Manager: Andre Cuello
Assistant Editor: Becky Golden-Harrell
Marketing Manager: Christine Degon
Cover Design: Cate Barr

Focal Press is an imprint of Elsevier
30 Corporate Drive, Suite 400, Burlington, MA 01803, USA
Linacre House, Jordan Hill, Oxford OX2 8DP, UK

 Recognizing the importance of preserving what has been written, Elsevier prints its books on
acid-free paper whenever possible.

Library of Congress Cataloging-in-Publication Data

British Library Cataloguing-in-Publication Data
A catalogue record for this book is available from the British Library.

ISBN: 0-2408-0753-7

For information on all Focal Press publications
visit our website at www.books.elsevier.com

05 06 07 08 09 10   10 9 8 7 6 5 4 3 2 1

Printed in the United States of America

**Working together to grow
libraries in developing countries**

www.elsevier.com | www.bookaid.org | www.sabre.org

ELSEVIER   BOOK AID International   Sabre Foundation

Contents

Introduction to Second Edition

The television industry, in recent years, has embraced the notions of branding as a means to survive and prosper in an ever-changing media marketplace. While the jargon of branding is now common throughout the business, few television professions have an in-depth knowledge of media brand management. This book provides the television executive with a succinct explanation of how the principles of brand management can be used to attract new viewers, promote audience loyalty and defend against competitive attacks. The second edition of this book addresses emerging branding issues not covered in the original text.

Since the publication of Branding TV in 1999, several industry trends have made the art and science of media brand management even more important. The first has been a dramatic increase in competition. Cable, satellite and the internet continue to flood the video marketplace with an increasing number of "channels" intended to attract audiences away from traditional broadcast television. A second trend has been ever-expanding digital technology that is blurring the boundaries among conventional media, such as newspapers, magazines, books, radio, television, cable, telephone, movies, and music recordings. This trend towards media convergence forces brand managers to think beyond the mere tangible or functional aspects of their media products and focus more on intangible and abstract perceptions. Additionally, the television industry's transition to digital provides technically more channels for program content and therefore, more branding challenges. Coinciding with this massive increase in channel capacity has been a similar increase in media-on-demand capabilities, such as TiVo and other personal video recording (PVR) devices, liberating audiences from rigid program schedules. A third trend has been the dramatic changes in media ownership, more commonly referred to as consolidation whereby managers and employees often work for more than one media outlet. Relaxation of ownership regulations has led to a series of corporate buyouts, mergers, partnerships, and strategic alliances. Media brand professions must juggle an array of interwoven brands. Taking this point a step further, another major industry trend has been the somewhat strained relationship between networks and their affiliated stations. As the networks or their corporate ownership continue to invest in alternative media, emerging business practices, such as "reverse compensation" and "repurposing" have caused many television station managers to reexamine their brand commitments to a parent network.

The intertwined impact of competition, convergence and consolidation has resulted in almost overwhelming choice and freedom for television audiences and advertisers, but this situation is not necessarily what people want. Brand researchers are finding that limitless options can reach a point of diminishing returns, where the "overloaded" human mind seeks out ways to simplify and uncomplicate decision-making. One common cognitive shortcut is to depend on *brand names*. We hope that the changes and additions to the second edition of this book will provide an updated and succinct explanation of television brand management

As the cover of this book declares, this work is designed specifically for television broadcasters. Although many of the media brand management principles presented can be applied to all electronic media, television offers a number of unique branding challenges. Furthermore, while the essential material found in this book can be applied to networks, stations and programs, it pays particular attention to the local commercial TV station and its news franchise. For instructional purposes, this seemed to be the most effective means of applying real-world examples for the majority of intended readers for this book.

The concepts of brand management and particularly brand equity are no more prevalent than in the battle for local news dominance, providing as much as 50 percent of a station's overall sales revenue. The financial payoff of a successful news operation can be enormous. For many stations, local news has become the only familiar and enduring brand asset.

Section one serves as an overview of basic principles of successful branding, concentrating on defining, measuring and managing media brand equity. Section Two takes these principles and translates them into practical executions in the real world of television broadcasting. To assist in the learning process, a hypothetical TV station and its struggling local news operation are incorporated into the final portions of the segment. Finally, we examine some important legal issues involved in protecting a brand and we attempt to say a few words about the future TV branding. We round out this volume with appendices dedicated to selected readings on brand management plus a practical guide on how to interpret a rating book.

Walter McDowell
Alan Batten
February 2005

About the Authors

Walter McDowell Ph.D. Before entering academia, Professor McDowell spent over two decades in commercial television, including station management positions in promotion, programming, and creative services. After earning his doctorate in Mass Communication from the University of Florida, and teaching for several years at Southern Illinois University, he joined the faculty of the School of Communication at the University of Miami in 2001. In addition to teaching various media management courses, Professor McDowell has published media branding studies in several academic publications including *The Journal of Media Economics*, and the *International Journal on Media Management*. A nationally known consultant, he also has authored two books published by the National Association of Broadcasters and Focal Press *Branding TV: Principles and Practices* (with Alan Batten) and *Troubleshooting Audience Research*.

Alan Batten. Alan Batten graduated from the University of Maryland (College Park) and undertook postgraduate work at Boston University's School of Public Communications. He has been active in the broadcast industry since 1971 where he had the opportunity to lead the marketing efforts of several stations affiliated with NBC, ABC, CBS, FOX and PBS. Along the way, he served as President of the Broadcast Promotion and Marketing Executives (now known as PROMAX). He has received countless industry awards and presented numerous international lectures on various aspects of broadcast marketing. In 1991, he founded ABCommunications to provide consulting services for marketing challenges. ABCommunications counts as clients such industry giants as Sinclair Broadcast Group, Universal Pictures, ACT III Broadcasting, and Raycom Sports. A writer at heart, he has written several motion picture and television scripts and enjoys producing radio commercials.

The Principles of Branding TV

PART 1

1 | Competition Changes Everything

Branding and many of the notions of brand management are not new to most American consumer goods. Some of today's most prominent brands, such as Coke, Levi, Maxwell House, Budweiser, Campbell, and Kellogg, began their branding efforts in the 1880s, when electronic media wasn't an industry or even an idea. What is new, however, is the adoption of branding and brand management by the electronic media. Radio and television broadcasters have for decades given unique "brand names" to their stations, networks, and programs, but the decade of the 1990s introduced a much deeper interest in the art and science of brand management.

The primary motivation for applying brand management to a consumer product or service is competition. As the number of similar products or services in the marketplace increases, the need for highly differentiated brands becomes more important. Also, with a rise in competition, there is usually a similar rise in the speed and sophistication of measuring brand performance in the marketplace. For retailers the introduction of technological marvels such as computerized UPC codes has enabled companies to almost instantly track consumer purchases for thousands of brands. And with this wealth of quick information comes the demand for quick brand performance. In an information-rich environment, impatient retailers don't hesitate to discard brands that don't deliver consistent and profitable sales. The same can be said for the survival of a television network or program in an ever-increasing competitive environment. The business of commercial broadcasting is the selling of audiences to advertisers, and in a world of overnight Nielsen ratings, impatient media executives do not hesitate to cancel programs that cannot deliver consistent and profitable audiences.

The late arrival of brand management to American television was due primarily to a lack of competition. For over three decades, the competitive arena for commercial television was restricted to three major players: ABC, CBS, and NBC. Through the interplay of various legal, economic, and technological factors, a three-network monopoly (or oligopoly) dominated the television industry from the 1950s to the mid 1980s. With this captive national audience, ABC, CBS, and NBC, as well as their affiliated stations, made huge profits with margins approaching 50 percent.

With so few stations licensed to each market, viewer choices were restricted to a handful of media brands. By the late 1980s, the competitive picture began to change when FOX became a legitimate network player, siphoning off young adult viewers from the "Big Three" networks. Although it didn't use the word "branding," FOX became the first broadcast network to stand for something in the minds of audiences. Its youthful, risky, irreverent style of program content set the stage for the industry's move to brand marketing.

The 1980s also witnessed the coming of age for cable television. Cable program networks such as CNN, ESPN, MTV, A&E, Nickelodeon, and Discovery began to encroach on the audience territory that was once the exclusive domain of the broadcast networks and their affiliated stations. As the number of unique cable programming options increased, so did the number of cable subscribers, and with more subscribers came more audience fragmentation. The talk of "branding" emerged in the mid 1990s when broadcast television began to lose sizable audiences to cable and other alternative media such as the Internet. At the beginning of the new century, with over 70 percent of U.S. households subscribing to digitally enhanced cable or satellite services, broadcasters can no longer count on captive audiences and guaranteed profits.

Complementing the important changes in media technology have been equally important changes in government regulation of electronic media. The Telecommunications Bill of 1996 and subsequent regulation changes fostered by the Federal Communications Commission (FCC) and Congress have stimulated market-driven competition by unshackling government restrictions on telecommunications. Broadcasting, cable, satellite, and telephone delivery systems all have the legal green light to cross boundaries and compete for consumers. Technological advances coupled with deregulation have begun to unleash a torrent of competition, which means audiences and advertisers have an abundance of choice.

It is important to remember that although media professionals may be enthralled with all the new technological "delivery systems" and economic "business models," the typical viewer is far more interested in content. The source of this content, whether it is local, syndicated, network, broadcast, cable, satellite, Internet, or cell phone, is of secondary importance. Research studies confirm that in an age of technological convergence, what counts is content or, more precisely, what the content does to satisfy the needs and desires of an audience. Consequently, successful media managers must change their focus from the pure hardware aspects of a media brand and concentrate more on the competition for ideas.

The dramatic rise in competition has led also to a reexamination of traditional program content theory. For example, prime-time programs for years were produced according to the least objectionable program (LOP) theory. The theory is based on the core idea of "moderate liking." Audience researchers discovered early on that most people do not watch television alone. Therefore, individual preference is often influenced by group dynamics in which extreme opinions, either positive or negative, are suppressed in favor of a group compromise. By definition, a compromise is a movement toward the common center or "lowest common denominator." This strategy might generate repeat customers for a program but not necessarily create highly committed fans. The LOP theory works well when there are few competitors, but as viewer options increase dramatically, programs designed for moderate liking can become a liability. Just as brand managers of many consumer goods have learned to market their products to highly targeted consumer segments, so media marketers are now obliged to aim program content at the specific needs of narrow, specialized audience segments. In a media environment with so much choice, trying to be all things to all people can no longer work. As will be shown later in this book, moderate liking is not the stuff of brand management.

Adding fuel to the fire of this emerging competitive marketplace is the fact that although the amount of program choice continues to increase, there has been no corresponding dramatic increase in the amount of time people spend watching television. Nielsen Media Research reports that over the past 15 years, the number of minutes per household dedicated to television viewing has remained almost unchanged. The disturbing implications for television programmers are that, although the number of slices in the programming pie has increased, the overall size of the pie itself has not changed appreciably. A number of media observers have referred to this phenomenon as media "cannibalism," in which program providers are forced into "feeding" on the audiences of fellow program providers. In brand marketing terminology, television viewing appears to have evolved into or zero sum, market in which the number of available customers for a product category is fairly stagnant. Therefore, as more brands enter the marketplace, the only means of survival is to take customers (audiences) away from the competition.

A further frustration for television executives is that despite the historic technological and regulatory breakthroughs that have freed audiences from supposedly too few choices, the typical viewer still prefers to deal with only a handful of channel options. Several studies indicate that for an average American household, there is a viewing threshold of only a dozen or so channels. For example, Nielsen Media Research conducts an annual national survey of television viewing characteristics, of which "channels received versus channels viewed" is a special section. Year after year the data reveal that, although the number of channels available to the home continues to grow, the number of channels actually viewed has hardly grown at all. Several academic researchers have used the concept of "channel repertoire" to describe this limited array of channels from which audiences select programming. This channel repertoire is similar in definition to what advertising researchers call a consideration set, whereby a consumer considers only a portion of the brands available in a purchase situation. In coming years, thanks to some new technology, these dozen channels will come even more entrenched in consumers' minds. Conventional remote controls are making way for more sophisticated filtering devises or "smart agents" that allow the viewer to preselect the most appropriate channels or programs, thus eliminating dozens if not hundreds of competing program sources. This notion is similar to an à la carte selection of program channels on subscription cable; something the cable industry is reluctant to adopt. Of course radio for years has confronted this problem in which an automobile radio push-button selector offers a predetermined a handful of stations for listening.

As if the above-mentioned audience behavior trends were not frustrating enough, broadcasters face the added problem that within this small set of a dozen or so preferred media brands, some brands are watched more often than others. That is, the sizes of the selected "slices" within the programming pie are not equal. To date, despite substantial losses in audiences ratings to cable in recent years, the major broadcast networks still maintain the largest share of viewing. But this share is diminishing.

By the late 1990s, many crystal ball gazers predicted that things would only get worse for the traditional television networks and their stations. One of the more pessimistic pundits talked of "the death knell for the broadcast networks" and claimed that the introduction of so much viewer choice was "a signal to the world that the old media empires are modern-day dinosaurs headed for extinction." This bleak Darwinian view has proven to be somewhat exaggerated. Instead of becoming extinct, many savvy media companies have taken inspiration rather than resignation from the notions of evolution and are adapting to their new surroundings. They are developing business strategies that will allow them to survive and prosper in the turbulent years to come. Some strategies involve exploiting new technologies, such as digital multicasting and Internet portals. Other strategies involve restructuring old business models, such as duopolies and cable partnerships. Still other survival strategies involve the adoption of brand marketing principles to attract and hold audiences.

1.1   BIRTH OF A BUZZWORD

In an effort to cope with unprecedented competition, audience fragmentation, and declining market shares, broadcasters and cable operators have looked to the highly competitive consumer goods industry for inspiration. The result has been the eager adoption of the jargon, if not always the substance, of brand management.

Media trade journals such as *Broadcasting and Cable, MediaWeek,* and *Advertising Age* have become more comfortable with the buzz of branding.

◆ A front-page banner headline in a trade magazine proclaims "Network Brand Marketing Fever."

◆ A major network places a full-page ad in an industry magazine boasting that it is "America's Leading Network Brand."

◆ In a published interview, a cable executive maintains that "any successful brand devotes resources to reinforcing its brand positioning."

◆ In a press release, a television network announces a new corporate position entitled Senior Vice President of Media Development, Brand Management, and Research.

◆ An advertisement for an off-network syndicated program insists that the program is "a proven brand with a loyal audience."

◆ Another ad for a new cable network contends that it is "taking branding to a whole new level."

◆ A programming executive reveals that high profile programs help "brand the Network identity."

◆ The headline for another trade article states that a media company "Will Build Its Brand in Originals."

◆ A classified employment ad seeks a Creative Director who will "steward the brand."

◆ A television critic congratulates the producers of a program for "establishing its own brand of show."

◆ A cover story on the future of cable discusses the notion of "bite-sized branding in a digital age."

◆ A headline in a *New York Times* article states that "television stations fear for their channel brand as choices proliferate in the digital age."

◆ A television network executive declares that "we want to make sure that the attitude and brand identity is cohesive throughout the day."

◆ A trade journalist reports from a Radio-Television News Directors' Association convention that "in an environment where decades-old network affiliations can be broken overnight, local newscasts remain the strongest and most stable form of brand equity."

◆ An editorial in a *Broadcasting and Cable* magazine states that "Branding has become the buzzword of the day . . . More is riding on the success or failure of broadcast branding than at any time in the medium's history." A later editorial states that "branding is threatening to supplant 'synergy' or 'convergence' as the queen bee of TV buzzwords."

Professional media associations, such as NATPE, PROMAX, NCTA, and CTAM have offered seminars on "The Branding Bug," "Our Brand New World," "Welcome to the Brand Revolution," "Branding Your Message to Win," "Cable Image Branding", and "Building a Reputation: Creating Brand Loyalty."

Although the media associations and trade press continue to make references to branding, brand identity, brand image, brand loyalty, and brand extensions, there has been a growing interest in that most muddled of brand management concepts, brand equity. Although there are dozens of definitions of brand equity offered by academia and the private sector, all experts would agree that equity stems from the added value a brand name contributes to a product's performance in the marketplace. For television broadcasters, performance means ratings and revenue.

For conventional consumer goods, strong brand equity is said to

◆ Reinforce consumer loyalty

◆ Attract new customers

◆ Protect a product from competitive attack

No wonder broadcasting and cable professionals have become absorbed with translating the principles of brand management into meaningful strategies for their media brands! But what is brand equity in the context of electronic media? And how does all that brand-marketing terminology—awareness, image, preference, positioning, etc.—contribute to the overriding concept of media brand equity? This book is intended to answer these questions and more.

2
CHAPTER

Branding is Just a Fancy Name for Promotion, Right?

Wrong.

Branding is more than that. Brand management has a special role within the larger context of promotion. Some promotion activities may have a branding component, whereas others may not. In simple terms, branding deals with a product's reputation. This encompasses those promotion activities that are intended to distinguish a brand from its competitors by communicating to consumers what the brand stands for. For media "products," this marketing communication can occur at several levels:

◆ On-air promos

◆ Advertising

◆ Public relations/publicity

◆ Product usage

In many cases, these levels can overlap to form an integrated marketing campaign (IMC). All of these communication tools will be discussed in detail in Section 2 of this book. What is important to remember here is that, despite the use of all of these marketing tools, promoting isn't always branding. For example, for a retailer, promoting discount pricing or coupons may stimulate short-term product sales but may do nothing for the brand's enduring reputation. In fact, some promotion activities may even hurt a brand's long term performance. Imagine if Mercedes Benz developed an inexpensive compact car for middle-income families and offered huge factory rebates. It would change the way one views the entire Mercedes Benz image. Promotion tools such as advertising and publicity would surely generate some dealer traffic, but what about the long-term consequences? In forthcoming months and years, will these types of promotion activities undermine the Mercedes brand? When affluent car buyers look for a prestigious luxury car, will they have second thoughts about this once proud brand?

The same situation can occur with the marketing and promotion of media brands. For example, a program's ratings success may be more the result of clever program scheduling or transitory promotion hype rather than genuine audience preference for the program. Does a "watch and win" contest generate audience sampling or merely short-lived audience "traffic" that disappears as soon as the contest ends? After the sweeps, will the program sustain its high ratings or sink like a rock? Effective media branding strategies are designed for the long run and make use of promotion techniques that will nurture audience loyalty. A conscientious media brand manager needs to look at his or her promotion efforts and ask a couple of important questions.

◆ Does this particular promotion effort enhance the long-term reputation of my brand?

◆ Does this promotion effort offer enduring reasons why my brand is superior to my competition?

Another common distinction between promotion and branding is that branding focuses more on the consumer, rather than on the product. Expanding on the idea is an often-overlooked description of what marketing professionals really do for a living. In the final analysis, successful marketers are not in the business of selling products but in the business of selling solutions to people's problems. These marketers ask how will the customer benefit from experiencing this product—"What's in it for me?" Smart marketers know that promoting the attributes of a branded product is only half the battle. A truly persuasive marketing message talks about the personal consumer benefits derived from these product attributes.

From this consumer-centered perspective, we can propose that Black and Decker is not so much in the business of selling power drills but rather in the business of responding to a consumer's need to create holes! Taking this example a step further into a genuine brand strategy, we can propose that Black and Decker is also selling its enduring reputation for precision and reliability. It is these more intangible brand associations that are the most difficult to copy by a competitor and typically form the bedrock of a strong brand.

Let's take a simple media example, an on-air promo for a local newscast. The promotion department produces a message that brags about its high-tech weather radar system and staff of meteorologists but fails to explain how these resources (or product attributes) will personally benefit viewers.

Which of the following copy phrases is more persuasive?

"Storm-Track Doppler Radar and our staff of meteorologists are ready for severe weather here in the heartland."

"Storm-Track Doppler Radar and our staff of experienced meteorologists are ready to protect you and your family from the dangers of severe weather."

The second copy example is more viewer-oriented and therefore generates emotion as well as information about the "product." Later we will see that the emotional or intangible components of a brand may be the only things that distinguish it from its market competitors.

An area in which both promoting and branding can run into trouble is the often misplaced emphasis placed on creativity. When creating any type of persuasive message, successful brand managers know that it's the ideas, not the glitz, that matter most. In other words, *marketing strategy should drive creativity*. Most promotion professionals are clever people, so a lack of creativity is rarely a problem. If anything, the problem is a creative overkill. Producers, copywriters, and artists sometimes are so consumed with getting people's attention that the creative "bells and whistles" ignore the original marketing objectives and strategies underlying the whole project. No one would deny that gaining an audience's attention is indeed a major achievement and that creativity is crucial for this particular task, but style should not be confused with substance. Consumer behavior research reveals time and again that, in addition to flashy graphics and music, consumers will also pay attention to a compelling message—a message that is grounded in consumer benefits. Creativity should be regarded as a means to an end, not an end unto itself. The Big Question for all creative people is "What are the compelling reasons why an audience will respond to this advertising or promotional message?"

Sergi Zyman, the outspoken author, consultant, and former guru for Coca-Cola, appreciates creative advertising but laments that so few advertising people will admit that advertising must be subservient to the goals of marketing. Here is how he defines marketing: "Marketing is a discipline, a science that positions your product in front of target consumers in relative terms to your competition. It has to present and explain and package and incite and insist the consumer buy more of your stuff instead of the other person's."

Too many creative "award winning" advertising and promo campaigns are long on entertainment but short on persuasion. In the above case, the terms *marketing* and *promotion* are essentially synonymous but are these efforts branding?

The bottom-line objective for any brand marketing effort should be to develop and nurture what many researchers and consultants call a sustainable competitive advantage, or SCA. From a branding perspective, the term sustainable is key and often what separates promoting from branding.

3 | Branding and the Marketing Mix

Although branding television is a relatively new field of study, the essential notions of brand management have been around for a long time and it would be foolish for broadcasters not to take advantage of the extensive research and expertise already available. The art and science of persuading people to buy something is not new; so instead of "reinventing the wheel" for ourselves, let's look at what is already known about brand management and modify these principles for our special media needs.

One of the essential tools used by most business schools and marketing organizations is the classic Marketing Mix, consisting of the following brand elements:

- Product
- Price
- Distribution (sometimes called "Place" to become part of the "Four P's of the Marketing Mix")
- Promotion

These marketing concepts can be adapted easily to a television broadcast environment.

3.1   PRODUCT

The product is the media content experienced by an audience. What better way to build a strong brand than to have the consumer use and appreciate the product. Following a satisfactory experience with the brand, positive thoughts and feelings will remain in the consumer's memory. Of course, a bad experience with the brand can lead to ruin. Brand marketing professionals know that nothing can ruin a great marketing plan quicker than a lousy product. Rather than squandering money and manpower on branding a poor product, it's better to overhaul the product and start over with a new brand name.

For television marketing executives, the "product" can be a network, a station, a program, or even a feature. This can be a tricky branding situation because these products can overlap so that one product is perceived as a distributor of another product. The reputation of a distributor can send a message about one or more of the branded products it makes available to consumers. For instance, what if Tiffany jewelry products were made available at all K-Marts? What if Winston cigarette products were added to the menu at McDonalds?

From a broadcasting perspective, program distributors, such as networks or stations, often have their own highly developed brands. Does a program airing on a FOX affiliate send a different message to an audience than the same program airing on a CBS affiliate does? To date, empirical research on this topic is minimal. However, a handful of studies suggest that, at least for typical television operations, the best branding opportunities remain at the program level. Cable, on the other hand, can often take a wider branding swing because of the continuity of programming offered by most cable networks.

3.2   PRICING

From a purely monetary vantage point, pricing is not a major concern for free over-the-air broadcasters. Even when broadcast stations are included on subscription cable services, research indicates that there is a general perception that the broadcast channels are essentially free. However, price can also be interpreted as the time invested in watching a program. A broadcaster wants the use of a media brand by an audience member to be time well spent and therefore, a good "investment."

Looking not too far to the digital future, there is much speculation that television broadcasters will someday enter the viewer subscription business, providing many niche-programming services to highly targeted audiences. In addition, the Internet will play an increasing role as an interactive device associated with television programming. If these scenarios unfold as predicted, television broadcasting will become more "retail," and pricing strategies for these new services will become a major concern.

Successful brands demonstrating high consumer-based brand equity can charge more for their products or services than can weaker brands. That is, consumers are more willing to pay a premium for a brand they know and appreciate.

3.3   DISTRIBUTION

For electronic media, controlling the distribution component of the marketing mix is more complex than for most consumer goods. First, there is the physical distribution of program content, which involves a station's signal strength and coverage contours. Cable and satellite retransmission would also come under this distribution aspect. It's impossible to nurture a strong media brand if audiences cannot see it! It is also misleading to brag about the supposed strength of a media brand when it has a competitive advantage in distribution. For example, historically UHF stations have suffered from signal deficiencies that, in turn, have impaired audience ratings. No amount of promotion can increase sales if potential customers are unable to buy the brand or tune into the programs.

An equally important distribution challenge involves program scheduling. Unlike most consumer goods, broadcast "products" are bound by time. Imagine a retail outlet in which the shelf displays changed every half hour to display different competing brands! The distribution of a media brand to consumers depends greatly on scheduling. Three important scheduling factors follow:

◆ HUTs (i.e., homes using television) levels
◆ Counter-programming
◆ Lead-in

Just as some consumer brands in a retail setting have better store locations or better shelf positioning, certain television programs are exposed to better audience "traffic" than are others. Each of the above factors can influence ratings performance (share of market) but not necessarily brand loyalty. Savvy brand managers know that all that glitters is not necessarily gold. As we will soon see, measuring the true strength (or equity) of a brand means *factoring out* marketing mix variables that can exaggerate the measured performance of a brand in a competitive marketplace.

3.4   PROMOTION

The final component of the traditional marketing mix is promotion, which includes communication activities aimed at informing, persuading, and reminding consumers about a particular brand. These activities include advertising, public relations, and sales promotions. Television networks and stations have an added advantage over retail goods in that they can use their own medium (on-air promos) to reach potential customers. What Proctor & Gamble pays millions of dollars to secure, television stations have at their disposal for free.

As mentioned earlier, not all promotion activity is branding. Most short-term promotion schemes intended to boost temporarily market shares seldom cultivate long-term brand loyalty. The true strength or equity of a consumer brand rests in its ability to attract and retain customers without succumbing to promotional gimmickry. Distracting consumers from the original "benefits package" of the brand implies that the marketer really doesn't believe in the inherent value of the brand.

In the quest for short-term ratings gains during the infamous Nielsen sweep weeks, television networks and stations for decades have resorted to a variety of programming and promotional tactics that are designed often to distort typical program performance. These tactics range from altering program schedules and manipulating story lines to massive advertising campaigns and on-air contests. Known by industry insiders as hyping, or hypoing, these practices have been condemned by Nielsen and various advertising organizations. Yet the practice continues. However, with the recent addition of so many metered "overnight" television markets, media buyers today can now look beyond the 4-week sweeps and evaluate long-term brand performance, which is the bread and butter of true brand management.

4 | Why People Like Brands

Before we attempt to untangle the exact meanings of all the latest branding buzzwords, let's first define the most basic of terms, a brand. The following is an all-purpose definition of a consumer brand taken from the American Marketing Association:

> A brand is a name, term, sign, design, or a unifying combination of them intended to identify and distinguish the product or service from its competitors. Brand names communicate attributes and meaning that are designed to enhance the value of a product beyond its functional value. The basic reason for branding is to provide a symbol that facilitates rapid identification of the product and its repurchase by customers.

These 68 words pack a lot of information. In fact, entire articles and book chapters have been written about some of the terms used with this concise definition.

Because consumers often lack the motivation, ability, or time to process all product information to which they are exposed, they look for quick solutions stored in their memory. Strong brands assist in this mental process. If consumers recognize a brand and have some knowledge about it, then they do not have to engage in a lot of additional thought or processing of information to make a product decision. Market researcher Alexander Biel offers the following insight:

> On a very practical level, consumers like brands because they package meaning. They form a kind of shorthand that makes choice easier. They let one escape from a feature-by-feature analysis of category alternatives, and so, in a world where time is an ever-diminishing commodity, brands make it easier to store evaluations.

4.1   BRANDS VERSUS CATEGORIES

At the core of all branding theory is the distinction between a product category and a product brand. A category refers to the generic commodity with no differentiation among brands. Depending on a number of motivational factors, a consumer may choose a category of product to satisfy a need with no consideration of brands—any brand will do. In another purchase situation, the same consumer may carefully evaluate the merits of a number of alternative brands—which is the best brand for me? A third option is the consumer seeks a specific brand with no consideration of category alternatives—only this brand will do.

In a cluttered marketplace, in which consumer products are often more similar than they are different, proper brand management increases the probability of consumer brand choice. Brand management is the reason why consumers want a Big Mac not just a hamburger, a pair of Nikes not just a pair of sneakers, a Harley rather than just a motorcycle. In media terms, we can say that media brand management is the reason why audiences tune to *Law and Order* rather than just any television drama, *Sex and the City* rather than just any television sitcom, *Eyewitness News* rather than just any local television newscast.

An important assumption for any practical measure of brand strength is that the brand under study should be a direct competitor coming from the same product category. In other words, mouthwashes should not be compared to deodorants, nor should television sitcoms be compared to newscasts.

4.2   BRANDS AND HABITS

Strong brands also cultivate habits. Researchers have found that in repetitive decision-making situations, habits save time and reduce the mental effort of decision making. For example, if the repeated outcomes resulting from the use of a branded product are positive, the likelihood of that consumer buying that brand again is increased. Human beings are creatures of habit because habits simplify our lives by reducing anxiety about taking chances.

If you are the brand manager of the incumbent leading brand, habitual behavior is a good thing because habits are really hard to break. For a brand challenger, however, consumer habits are the enemy. Instead of examining and conscientiously evaluating each brand, habitual buyers simply bypass all this effort and retrieve from memory a preferred brand and hand over the money! Media brands experience the same dilemma. Once established, daily or even weekly viewing habits are extremely hard to break. For example, the biggest problem that broadcasters face during fall premiere weeks is persuading audiences to break old habits and sample new programming.

Viewers who cannot discern any compelling reason to change channels will tend to remain tuned to the channel that is already in use. A typical example is the late evening newscast block in which three or four stations go head to head with highly similar program content. More often than not, the most influential factor in determining a newscast's share of audience will be the share of its lead-in program. This implies that many viewers see all newscasts as equally satisfying and therefore not worth changing stations.

In the best of marketing circumstances, people like brands because they save time, energy, and risk when purchasing a product or service. Once a preferred brand has been set up in memory, the purchase decision becomes automatic or habitual. In fact, a consumer will go out of his or her way to seek out this best of all brands. In the worst of circumstances, all competing brands are considered satisfactory and the purchase decision is based more on chance than choice.

5 | Sales Promotion as Branding

For media brands operating under an advertising-based business model, branding should be a two-fold process addressing both audience and advertising brand equity goals. Although the most visible forms of marketing and promotion are aimed at the general public to attract audiences, the business community, represented by advertisers and media buyers, is equally important. In fact, it is this second group that ultimately buys the brand and generates revenue. Although audience-based branding strategies are aimed primarily at the general public, often segmented into narrower demographic or lifestyle groupings, advertiser-based branding strategies concentrate on a much smaller audience of business decision makers possessing special knowledge.

From a conceptual standpoint, these dual efforts often share little in common, requiring managers and employees to reconcile these differences into an integrated branding mindset.

An important question is to what extent should the two branding strategies overlap and to what extent should they diverge and become independent projects? In other words, that which persuades audiences to watch or listen may not persuade advertisers to buy. One can assume that media buyers are aware of audience-branding strategies simply because they are exposed to the same advertising and promotional tactics as the general public. Furthermore, these audience-attracting efforts help advertisers better understand the types of potential customers that might be watching. However, this audience-brand knowledge is not sufficient to build and maintain advertiser-based brand equity. The media-advertiser business relationship might include components that have little or no connection with audiences. For example, a station sales department may want to build an exceptional reputation for client service, emphasizing trust, promptness, and reliability, things that go beyond ratings and cost-per-thousands.

When selling a program package to a potential advertiser, there should be a sense of a coherent brand identity that may encompass the network, the station, and the individual programs. This challenge implies more than just organizing properly the tangible assets of a company. It also means dealing with human assets and the intangibles of branding. Employees must buy into the brand "ideology" of their employer, often referred to as the corporate culture. According to renowned brand researchers Leslie McEnally and Malcolm de Chernatony, brand management requires a corporate culture in which

> Employees must understand the brand's vision, its core values . . . and perform in a manner consistent with the brand's identity and be empowered to take actions that enhance it . . . This requires extensive training and a comprehensive explanation of the brand's meaning and strategy.

Note how the terms vision, core values, identity, and meaning all depict knowledge of a brand that transcends ordinary functional attributes of the product or service. For a television station promoting its *Eyewitness News* brand, there should be a well-conceived integrated branding strategy that includes both audience-based and advertiser-based elements. Regrettably, for many stations audience and advertiser marketing efforts have been delegated to different departments, typically the promotion and sales departments. A few stations have seen the light of a unified media brand management strategy and have combined responsibilities under the supervision of a single department head. For the remainder of Section I of this book, most of the discussion can be applied to both audience and sales branding efforts.

6 | Say What You Mean, Mean What You Say: The Jargon of Brand Management

CHAPTER

Although branding experts have yet to reach perfect agreement on the definitions of some of these concepts, media professionals and media journalists have been the worst offenders. They often use the following branding terms interchangeably. Here is a brief clarification of some common terms.

By depicting a program as a *product* and an audience member or advertiser as a *consumer*, most branding concepts can be adapted readily to broadcasting.

6.1 BRANDING

Branding is the process of naming a product or service in order to distinguish it from its category competitors. In broadcasting a brand name would be the name of a network, station, or program. For example, *Eyewitness News* is a branded local newscast. However, true branding is more than attaching a name to a product or service. The intent of branding is to make the brand name something unique, memorable, and valuable in the minds of consumers.

6.2 BRAND EXTENSION

Brand extension is the process of branding a new product with an already established brand name. The marketing premise for this action is that the established brand has valuable branding assets that can be transferred to the new product. Positive thoughts and feelings that consumers have about the original product will hopefully carry over to the new product.

An example would be Ford creating a new type of automobile or truck but still identifying it as a Ford product. For electronic media, some examples of a brand extension would be creation of an additional prime-time news magazine on CBS called *60 Minutes II* or the creation of a cable channel called MSNBC that capitalizes on the reputations of two familiar corporations. On the local level, extending the *Eyewitness News* brand name to all newscasts airing on a station would be considered a brand extension.

The one note of caution when dealing with brand extensions is that the two products must have something in common. Adding the Ford brand name to a new kitty litter product doesn't make sense, nor would adding the *Eyewitness News* brand name to a new half-hour game show. There are many case studies in which a poorly conceived brand extension has actually hurt the stature of the original brand. In this era of ownership duopolies (and triopolies!) and extended digital channels (multicasting), this notion of brand extension will become a vital issue for station management.

6.3   BRAND AWARENESS

Brand awareness (or brand identity) is the first rung on the brand equity ladder. It refers to the simple familiarity (recall or recognition) of a brand relative to its product category. In electronic media terms, this could be the simple recall or recognition of a network, station, or program name or logo.

When all brands under consideration are thought to be equally satisfying, top-of-mind awareness becomes extremely important in brand marketing. This narrower view of awareness looks only at the brands that are recalled first by a consumer (or audience member). Experimental studies have confirmed that simple top-of-mind brand awareness can be the deciding factor in choosing a brand. Top-of-mind recall is sometimes measured by what researchers call *accessibility from memory*, meaning that in a purchase situation, some brand names are more likely to be "accessed" than are other brands. This heightened awareness of certain brands is often the result of heavy exposure to advertising.

6.4   BRAND INVOLVEMENT

Brand involvement is the degree of "consumer energy" invested in a purchase decision. Some product purchases are more involving than are others. For instance, buying an expensive new car is far more involving than is buying a cheap tube of toothpaste. Branding is extremely important in low involvement situations because the consumer is unwilling to invest a lot of time and energy in evaluating all the available brands.

Most television viewing is considered a low involvement activity, in which the media consumer seldom agonizes over what network or program to watch. Consequently, our prior concept of top-of-mind awareness becomes a critical branding consideration. If the viewer is not motivated to do a thorough analysis of each brand (low involvement) and if, on the surface, all available brands appear to offer the same level of satisfaction, top-of-mind awareness can drive the channel "purchase."

6.5   BRAND IMAGE

Brand image goes beyond awareness and deals with the meaning or reputation of the brand, where the consumer describes a cluster of thoughts and feelings. These different meanings are often referred to by brand researchers as brand associations. Some researchers compare *brand associations* in terms of their relative favorability, strength, and uniqueness.

From an electronic media perspective, audiences can be asked what thoughts and feelings come to mind when a particular network, station, program or on-air talent is mentioned. Once analyzed properly, this qualitative information can be distilled into specific brand dimensions that can used in positioning the relationship of our target brand to its direct competitors.

6.6   BRAND ATTITUDE

Brand attitude can be viewed as an extension of brand image in that the term refers not only to thoughts and feelings about the brand but evaluations and, most importantly, predispositions to respond (purchase). In other words, although brand image asks what you know and feel about the brand, brand attitude asks what is your appraisal of the brand. How strong are your intentions to buy the brand? Some brand researchers merge *brand image* with *brand attitude* and use either term.

Television audiences can evaluate a program and develop a predisposition to watch or not. Later, we will see how stubborn consumer brand attitudes can be. Rarely can a television program reinvent itself after bombing during its first few episodes. "Once a turkey, always a turkey" is in the minds of most media consumers.

Here again, the idea of reputation works well. You can know a lot about a person and have certain emotions associated with this knowledge. Consequently, you probably have formed an attitude based on what you have experienced; all of which are the ingredients of a reputation. It seems plausible that we can also assign a reputation to a television network or program.

6.7   BRAND PREFERENCE

Brand Preference is synonymous with a positive brand attitude. Based on their thoughts, feelings, and resultant evaluation of competing brands, consumers will, hopefully, have one they prefer over all others. Again, satisfaction drives preference. For many low-involvement consumer goods, including television programs, we know that there is often no strong brand preference. In these ambivalent situations, "brand promiscuity" takes over in which the final brand choice is driven by factors other than the brands' stellar reputation.

Within a broadcasting context, we can imagine a situation in which a program is not necessarily preferred but is the lucky recipient of a huge lead-in. Is the viewer's decision to watch a matter of preference or mere chance? An exception to this behavior would be an "appointment program," in which, despite being carried along within a huge lead-in, the viewer changes channels in order to watch a preferred brand of programming.

6.8   BRAND POSITIONING

Brand positioning lies at the heart of all brand marketing and is defined here as the image of a brand defined in relationship to its market competitors. Competing brands can be positioned according to any number of brand associations. By using quantitative survey data, researchers will often use "perceptual mapping" to graphically present the relative position of each competing brand. When a brand is analyzed from a more statistical point of view, such as perceptual mapping, brand associations are often called dimensions.

In most business situations, the goal for a brand manager is to "position" a brand so that it has a highly distinctive (differentiated) image in comparison to brands offered by competitors. However, there can be an opposite circumstance in which a new or struggling brand needs to be positioned as highly similar to "the leading brand." A new brand may be priced much lower than the competition, and all the manufacturer wants is to have consumers believe that, in terms of benefits, the new brand is essentially the same as the leading brand—only cheaper. Similarly, the owner of a media brand, such as a new local television news franchise, may be more than happy to have news viewers believe that, compared with its established competitors, the new entry is equally satisfying. Conversely, more aggressive broadcasters may discover through research some vulnerability in the competition and accordingly position their new program as distinctive and more valuable than the old tried-and-true program already airing.

As with most brand terminology, brand positioning dimensions should be consumer-centered, meaning that what is most important is how customers think and feel about the brand. Remember, we are talking about psychological positioning, not a count of news vans, bureaus, helicopters, and weather radar units. This means getting outside the boardroom and investing in meaningful audience research. This research will be the foundation on which you will build the branding efforts.

6.9   BRAND TRIAL

Brand trial (or brand sampling) is the initial purchase or experience with a brand by a consumer. Manufacturers may offer incentives to try a new brand, such as free samples, discount pricing, coupons, or contests. Broadcasters have a number of incentive tools to accomplish the same goal. A growing debate within the industry is that broadcasters are exploiting promotional incentives, such as contests, to pump up Nielsen ratings during critical sweep weeks. Within the context of television branding, promotional "incentives" should encourage sampling, whereby these new viewers remain with the program after the incentives are withdrawn.

6.10   BRAND CHOICE

Brand choice is the measure of actual consumer behavior within the competitive marketplace. This behavior may or may not be connected to preference. For example, you may prefer to drive a new Lincoln Explorer to work, but instead you choose to drive a used Ford Fiesta because you cannot afford the payments on the Lincoln.

A brand may be chosen because it is the only brand available. This exclusivity is great for sales and market share but can be misleading when looking for genuine brand preference. Similarly, a television program may be chosen because it is the only one of its type available during a certain time period. In addition, a program may be chosen because it is on the receiving end of a big lead-in. In terms of true preference, the available audience may be completely indifferent but simple inertia keeps them on the same channel. Conversely, a program may be preferred but seldom chosen because of intervening factors, such as the availability to watch or group (family) pressure to watch something else.

6.11   BRAND LOYALTY

Brand loyalty can be defined in two ways. The first and more common definition merges psychological and behavioral factors to measure a consumer's faithfulness to a brand in that mere repeat purchases are seen as an indicator of loyalty. The second approach, and the one selected for this book, makes a distinction between behavior and attitudes. Within this context, brand loyalty is a measure of consumer behavior only—the degree of repeat purchases to the exclusion of other brands.

Repeat purchases may or may not be a result of strong, positive attitudes or preference. As with our definition of brand choice, brand loyalty can also be coercion, in which the consumer has no options or is influenced by marketing mix factors that masquerade as faithfulness.

Television is very much a repeat business, and as a result, habitual behavior is important to understand. Some brand researchers have looked to the world of physics to help explain this ritualistic behavior. They maintain that repeat purchases of a brand can be characterized as inertia. A typical definition of inertia is that it is the property of matter that manifests itself as a resistance to change in the motion of a body. Thus when no external force is acting, a body at rest remains at rest and a body in motion continues moving in a straight line.

From a perspective of consumer behavior, we can define our consumer as the "body" and the forces of inertia as those marketing factors that encourage "resistance to change" or habit. To have the body change direction, there must be an adequate "external force," which can be defined as a competing brand. The concept of inertia is referred to in several marketing and mass communication studies. Long ago, broadcasters realized that the reason people watch a program often depends simply on its lead-in program. This audience carryover effect is sometimes referred to as "tuning inertia" or "inheritance effects," implying that much of a program's loyalty is inherited rather than earned.

Long-term viewing habits can be based on factors other than a real love affair with the media product. Perhaps somebody is a "loyal" viewer of a 10:00 p.m. newscast not because it is deemed the best but because it is the only 10:00 p.m. newscast in the market! This loyalty in behavior may disguise a real dissatisfaction with the content of the program.

6.12   BRAND SATISFACTION

Brand satisfaction is associated directly with trial and usage in that it is the evaluative result of experiencing a brand. In this respect, the term resembles aspects of brand attitude, but satisfaction is grounded in the idea of consumer expectations, which lie at the heart of brand management. Brand satisfaction asks the following question: "Does this brand live up to its promises?" Logically, satisfaction drives commitment, which in turn drives loyalty.

Studies have found that Americans today are fairly satisfied with most consumer products. Brand managers continue to face the challenge of stopping customers from defecting to competing brands that are seen to be of similar function and value. Instead of investing time and mental effort seeking a specific brand, they select the product that is (1) most familiar, (2) most available, or (3) least expensive.

6.13   BRAND COMMITMENT

Brand commitment is the psychological bedrock of branding that addresses the underlying psychology of brand loyalty. Where loyalty is a measure of consumer behavior, brand commitment is a measure of the degree of faithfulness to a brand despite counter-programming, lead-ins, contests, or other competitive maneuvers designed to lure consumers away. For example, highly committed customers will be willing to pay a higher price for a brand that they truly believe is superior. In electronic media terms, a truly committed viewer will seek out a specific program. Later we will see that the fundamental cause of brand equity is this core psychological relationship of commitment for which repeat viewing (loyalty) is the desired outcome. Consumer inertia implies that there are non-committed consumers who can be motivated to choose a brand by simply controlling marketing mix factors that have little to do with a brand's perceived value.

6.14   BRAND EQUITY

Brand equity is the power of a brand name. It is the added value a brand name brings to a product or service to motivate consumers to buy—or watch. An underlying assumption of any brand equity theory is that if you took the brand name away, consumers will behave differently. Imagine the changes in consumer purchasing if the brand name "Coke" were taken away from that cola product and substituted with "Go-Go Cola" or simply "generic cola drink." Imagine the changes in retail sales if the name "Nike" and its distinctive swoosh logo were removed from all its sneakers. Imagine the golden arches being dismantled in favor of a neon sign that says "Hamburgers Sold Here." From a media perspective, imagine informing the people at NBC that they must change the name of their *ER* to *Medical Drama.*

Brand equity takes a brand beyond its generic product category and makes it special by emphasizing its enduring reputation. Furthermore, this reputation should address consumer benefits that go beyond mere functional characteristics if for no other reason than functional characteristics are often so easy for competitors to copy; you buy a helicopter, so they buy a helicopter. You buy Doppler radar, so they buy Doppler radar. Because brand equity is the holy grail of brand management, we have given the concept its own chapter.

Again, what sets apart brand equity from other marketing concepts is that knowledge of the brand name alone is identified as the causal factor in altering consumer responses to marketing activities. In fact, many studies have found that the marketing mix strategies mentioned earlier are more effective when working with a strong brand name. In this respect, strong brands become shortcut devices for simplifying decision making. Brand-conscious consumers do not burden themselves with extensive cognitive effort. Instead, they rely on brand knowledge stored in memory to make quick, stress-free purchase decisions.

The enemy of brand equity is the notion of equivalent substitutes, wherein several competing brands are perceived by the consumer as equally satisfying. Under these conditions of no genuine brand differentiation, businesses often succumb to mutually destructive marketing battles, such as pricing wars, and extravagant but ineffectual advertising campaigns.

CHAPTER 7

TV Brand Equity: Why Brand Equity Is a Good Thing for TV

Although brand management had been on the American business scene for decades, the specific topic of brand equity did not become popular until the volatile 1980s, when once proud brands such as Sears, IBM, and Cadillac began to lose ground to lower-priced generic competition. Market shares dropped as a serious nationwide recession further aggravated corporate profits. This historic economic downturn inspired a rash of company consolidations and "downsizing" actions. Prudent cost cutting is indeed one way to shore up sagging profit margins, but as Sears' CEO, Arthur Martinez, warned at the time, "You can't shrink your way to greatness." Brand building is essential for growth.

During many leveraged buyout negotiations, corporate executives and Wall Street investors had to come to terms with the portfolio value of brand names. The recognition of brands as valuable intangible assets fostered an increased interest in brand equity as a topic for private and scholarly research.

The initial success of less expensive generic brands during the 1980s implied that consumers were failing to acknowledge the supposed added value of a "name brand" commodity and were influenced more by factors such as pricing and shopping convenience. This added value that immunizes a brand from such competitive incursions is often referred to as its equity. Businesses coping with "mature" product categories that exhibit little or no growth are particularly interested in brand equity. In such cases, competitive pressures are intense as sales gains (share increases) are derived from competitors rather than new category users. Under these zero-sum circumstances, as the number of competitors increase, the battle for market share becomes more acute.

In a single phrase, brand equity is a good thing because successful consumer brands tend to remain successful. This momentum in market performance is revealed in a brand's stability and predictability over time. It is easy to identify many retail brands with amazing "staying power" that have been market leaders in their respective product categories for decades: Kodak, Goodyear, Nabisco, Gillette, and, of course, Coke. Similarly, not only do popular television programs draw bigger audience shares, but these shares are fairly consistent over time. Abrupt changes in market rank occur more often among weaker challengers than with the established market leader. And if a leading brand does experience a drop in performance, it is usually a gradual deterioration over many months or years.

Weaker brands are more volatile and take brand managers on unwelcome roller coaster rides. For the television industry, this is a familiar phenomenon during the critical fall premiere weeks when audiences sample and abandon new shows on a nightly basis. On the other hand, strong returning programs, such as *Law and Order*, appear often to "ride out the storm" with minimal fluctuations in ratings. This is a bonus to strong brand equity; weaker programs don't enjoy the "sample-proof" performance. After a few weeks, the unsubstantiated hype takes its toll, with only a tiny handful of new programs being declared "breakthrough hits."

A second advantage of strong brand equity is that it can be used to support brand extensions. The added value of a brand name can be assigned to a new product line, giving the product a marketing boost in consumer acceptance. A successful media brand can buttress the promotion of another program or network. The names MSNBC, *60 Minutes II*, and ESPN 2 were not created by accident. Each capitalized on the reputation of an established consumer brand. Probably the most dramatic brand extensions for broadcasters in recent years involve the creation of internet portals, specialized Web sites, and digital multicasting projects.

Third, consumer brands with high equity are more cost-effective to promote. Struggling brands need proportionately more promotion than do successful brands to attract and hold customers. Furthermore, research has found that advertising messages for highly successful brands tend to be more believable than are similar messages emanating from new or struggling brands. This phenomenon goes back to our earlier discussions of brand familiarity and attitude persistence, in which consumers remain stubborn in their beliefs regardless of the quality of arguments presented by competing brands. The bottom line is that to achieve the same branding goals, brand challengers must invest more time, money, and effort work in marketing mix activities than do brand leaders.

Television marketing professionals can experience the same financial fruits of strong brand equity, particularly when initiating advertising campaigns. Holding the promotional high ground with a successful program is far easier than fighting the uphill battle of changing people's established attitudes and viewing habits.

Finally, strong brand equity is a good thing because of "the rule of double jeopardy" found in most retail consumer goods and television programs. For decades, researchers have confirmed that the most popular brands (largest market shares) also cultivate the most loyal customers. The double jeopardy rule influences smaller brands in that not only do they have fewer customers but these customers tend not to be as loyal in terms of repeat purchases. Even in this era of niche marketing, the notion of a "small but loyal" customer base (or audience base) is extremely rare in the real world.

Researchers have found that this loyalty advantage is a trait found not in the heavy users of a product category but in the light users—consumers who purchase a product occasionally. Heavy users of a product tend to "shop around," looking for variety and new experiences. Light users, on the contrary, tend to remain faithful to one brand, and that one brand is usually the market leader. Over the course of several weeks or months, the cumulative effect of these "soft core" buyers begins to show in market shares.

From a television branding perspective, bigger is also better. Studies indicate that the most popular programs also have proportionately more loyal audiences than do less popular shows. In addition, this loyalty is more common among infrequent users of a media product. For example, people who watch local news only once or twice a week tend to watch the same newscast, and that newscast usually is the market leader.

Of course, being on top doesn't guarantee long-term brand survival. One can find dozens of case histories in which established market leaders have fallen out of grace. Brand equity can be a perishable commodity when ignored or abused. For over 30 years, the number one luxury car in America was the Packard.

8 | Learning from Radio

Experiencing massive competition long before television began to feel the competitive heat from cable and satellites, the radio industry began to experience a competitive upheaval in the late 1970s, when the Federal Communications Commission (FCC) introduced hundreds of new AM and FM frequency allocations. Since that time, the commission periodically has opened up more and more spectrum.

Radio broadcasters may not have used the term branding until the 1990s, but the fundamental ideas behind brand equity have been in play by radio managers for many years. As a result, radio professionals are already successful at using some basic tenets of brand marketing. Ideas regarding audience segmentation and brand positioning have been staples of radio programming and promotion. Skillful radio operators attempt to position themselves in the minds of target audience segments as truly unique and valuable compared with their competitors. Following through on this positioning process, radio people also appreciate the adage "you can't be all things to all people." In branding, there is an inevitable trade-off in targeting audience segments. The good news is that you will have the opportunity to nurture highly enthusiastic and loyal audiences. The bad news is that there will be some audience segments within the marketplace that will never listen to your radio station.

Two branding lessons television can learn from radio are as follows:

(1) The more unique and superior your programming content, the more likely a station will cultivate audience loyalty. Radio programmers want to instill in their audiences the fear that if they tune away, they are going to miss something worthwhile—something that can not be found elsewhere. This could be a favorite song, a joke or outrageous comment by the disc jockey, or something as mundane as school closings and traffic reports. The worst situation occurs when the listeners perceive two or three stations to be essentially the same in terms of listener benefits (satisfaction). Then, the slightest provocation, such as a commercial or a less-then-perfect song title, will encourage audiences to defect. Media brand equity keeps listeners tuned in.

(2) Properly branded radio stations tend to remain prosperous over the long run. In other words, success breeds success. Take a look at the Arbitron

ratings of the top-ranked stations in any market and you will discover that most have remained in that top tier for years. Earlier we discussed how effective branding generates a kind of consumer momentum that protects the brand from competitive attack. This momentum can be construed as its brand equity. Of course, spectacular turn-around scenarios do occur among some underperforming radio stations, but these cases are the exception rather than the rule and therefore make headlines in the trade magazines.

8.1   RADIO IS NOT TV

Although there are many similarities between radio and television, there are significant differences, particularly in the areas of programming and audience behavior, which can influence branding strategies.

Although television tends to be divided into strict half-hour or 1-hour program units offering different program content, radio tends to work with long 4-hour dayparts with consistent program content. In fact, radio stations often maintain the identical "sound" throughout the entire broadcast day (e.g., a classic rock station is unlikely to switch formats to light jazz during the day). Compare this to a typical television network affiliate that begins its day with news/talk followed by afternoon soaps, followed by early fringe sitcoms, followed by local and network news, followed by game shows in prime access, and followed by an array of primetime magazines, dramas, and sitcoms and culminating in late news and late night talk/variety! Because of this continual change in program content, it is extremely difficult to brand effectively a television station, whereas a radio station presents better branding opportunities.

Of course, there are some obvious television exceptions to this handicap. Today, many cable networks, such as CNN, MTV, The Comedy Network, and ESPN demonstrate a continuity of program content that makes branding easier.

Associated with the dissimilar programming formats, there is a corresponding difference in audience behavior between the radio and television. Television audiences tend to tune in at specific times (on the hour or half-hour) and stay with a program. "Joining in progress" (JIP) is a rarity. Radio, on the other hand, can handle tune-in audiences at almost any minute during the day but is vulnerable to audiences abandoning the station at any moment. This is why radio operators place so much emphasis on Arbitron *cume* and *turnover* data. Again, many cable channels have adopted a radio-inspired program format.

Another important difference lies in the audience perceptions of stations, networks, and programs. Although many radio stations are affiliated with one or more networks, most listeners are not particularly aware of this fact or find it unimportant overall. In an effort to maintain "localism," radio stations tend not to promote their network affiliations. Television audiences, however, are becoming ever more aware of their network partners. This phenomenon began in the late 1980s with the introduction of the FOX network as an obvious programming alternative to the Big Three. Since then, other upstart networks such as UPN, WB, PAX, and Telemundo have attempted to project specific imagery that sets them apart from their competitors. Even the more established ABC, CBS, and NBC networks have in recent years tried to enhance viewer awareness by persuading their affiliated stations to adopt network slogans, music, and graphics for local and syndicated program promotion efforts. This network-station branding dilemma will be discussed in more detail later in the book.

Unlike radio, television programming consists of dozens of distinct program units, each with a specific brand name. Studies indicate that television viewers are far more familiar with programs than they are with the station identity (call letters or channel) or its affiliated network. In many cases, the subjects attribute the wrong station or the wrong network to some of their favorite programs. This confusion rarely occurs among radio audiences. The long-form consistency of radio programming is more conducive to branding a station. While television still appears reluctant to narrow its programming options during the course of a typical broadcast day, there will remain the daunting challenge of creating a singular, cohesive brand identity.

9 | Building TV Brand Equity

In Chapter 6, we clarified the working definitions of several branding terms. A larger issue is that many of these definitions overlap to some degree. For example, brand attitude and brand preference share many elements, as do brand loyalty and brand commitment. Defining all-important television brand equity can be frustrating because it includes components of all of these concepts. So let's simplify things!

We have adopted a straightforward equity framework proposed by brand scholar and consultant Kevin Keller of the Tufts School of Business at Dartmouth College. We can define television brand equity as the differential effect a brand name has on the audience response to a program (network or feature). The term differential means that audiences will respond differently, depending on their knowledge of a branded product or service. A television brand is said to have positive brand equity when audiences react more favorably to a program when the brand is identified than when it is not. This brand-driven loyalty is reflected in various ways, including audience perceptions, preferences, and behavior. Television brand equity depends ultimately on what resides in the minds of audiences. We can separate this concept into *brand awareness* and *brand image*.

Brand awareness is defined in the identical manner as our earlier presentation of common branding jargon. That is, awareness is the ability of an audience member to identify properly a brand through recognition or recall.

Brand image deals with the meaning of a brand and addresses brand associations (thoughts and feelings) stored in memory. Other branding concepts, such as brand attitude, brand preference, and brand commitment, can all be placed under this image concept. In addition, brand image can be evaluated from three perspectives:

◆ Strength—how strong are the brand associations?

◆ Favorability—how desirable are the brand associations?

◆ Uniqueness—how different are the brand associations?

If a brand demonstrates a weakness in any of these areas, there is a problem.

Using the above definition of brand equity, the following is a discussion of research-based strategies designed to help build powerful media brands, especially for television. Remember that promotion is not necessarily branding. The objective of these brand-building recommendations is to achieve sustainable strategic advantage based on the factors of awareness and image.

9.1 PART I

9.1.1 Building Brand Awareness

The first phase in equity building is enhancing the familiarity of the brand with media consumers. The notion of awareness implies memory functions. To recall or recognize a brand name means that it has been retrieved from a person's long-term memory. Enabling people to remember something is our task here, and we can borrow several proven strategies from psychology and education.

9.1.2 Reach Builds Awareness

To have brand awareness in a competitive market, you must reach a sufficient number of potential customers.

Media planners have yet to formulate the perfect reach and frequency plan for all brands. For many years frequency took precedence, but recently computer-driven media buying strategies place more emphasis on the cumulative audience reached. Depending on the desired target audience, this process can often be achieved using strategically placed on-air promos. However, a station or network may need to use additional media to accomplish this goal.

The most compelling branding message will have little impact if it does not reach the intended consumer. Reaching a target audience does not always require advertising. Well-conceived public relations activities and even some sales promotions can be an effective tool for reaching people.

9.1.3 Frequency Builds Awareness

Repetition, repetition, repetition! When learning a new language, the best way to memorize important words and phrases is to say the phrases over and over again. On the most fundamental level of marketing, many brand campaigns have failed merely because of a lack of frequency. Although reach is indeed important, a target audience must receive a branding message more than once, and therefore, reach alone is not a good predictor of brand awareness.

Frequency cannot be adequately determined without introducing another important variable: time. Marketing and advertising researchers have found that the interval between exposures is as important as the mere number of brand exposures. For example, an advertising campaign consisting of 10 ads over a span of 1 week will have more consumer impact than the same 10 ads distributed over a month.

Frequency can also be enhanced through public relations and sales promotion activities.

9.1.4   Consistency Builds Awareness

Suppose some McDonald's restaurants had a golden arch, and others did not. Suppose some Ford truck commercials ended with the slogan "Ford Tough," and others ended with "Affordable Ford." Suppose a station's local news franchise applied a different name and slogan for each newscast. Along with high frequency comes the need to be consistent or uniform in your branding message.

Regardless of the number or variety of promos, there are certain brand dimensions that must always be present. These crucial awareness-building items include, but are not limited to graphics, music, slogans, and the overall mood or demeanor of the message. These messages must be uniform over time. Changing branding tactics every few months is not effective branding, particularly if key ingredients of a brand's identity are changed. Do you really want to take down those golden arches and erect something "new and fresh"? Broadcasters are particularly guilty of knee-jerk change whenever ratings take a dip. If there is a real or imagined problem with local news performance, unenlightened managers suddenly change the jingle, change the logo, change the set, and change an anchor or two. This periodic desecration of a brand's identity is brand management at its worst.

An ongoing branding debate among station operators involves how closely they want to be associated with their network. Of course, network O&O stations are compelled to fall in line with their parent company, but there are hundreds of affiliates that are not willing clones, especially when the networks have fallen on hard times. From an on-air perspective, it is impossible to divorce one's station from a network, but stations can, to some degree, strike out on their own to create a more "localized" brand.

9.1.5   Simplicity of Execution Builds Awareness

The best logos have the fewest elements (e.g., the Nike swoosh logo is considered marketing classic). The best slogans have the fewest words (e.g., Nike's "Just Do It"). A rule of thumb for creative producers is: the fewer number of parts, the more readily an object can be remembered. This "less is more" approach does not mean that the original message should be superficial or unsophisticated. On the contrary, a common creative challenge for brand managers is making a complex idea simple to understand. For example, Prudential's long-standing "Piece of The Rock" campaigns address the often-complicated world of financial security with a simple yet powerful logo and slogan. Building brand awareness for electronic media requires the same emphasis on simplicity and memorability. Even in this high tech age of glowing digital read-outs, CBS's *60 Minutes* retains with a vengeance its simple wind-up stopwatch logo with its unmistakable "tick, tick, tick" audio signature.

9.1.6   Exposures from Multiple Sources Builds Awareness

Educational psychologists have confirmed that if the same message is received from a variety of sources rather than a single source, learning is enhanced. The message for brand marketers is "don't spend all your advertising dollars on one medium." One hundred thousand dollars spent on a combination of radio, newspaper, and outdoor advertising will be more effective in nurturing brand awareness than investing the entire budget in any one medium. This phenomenon is related to our earlier discussions of reach and frequency in that a target audience can be "reached" through several media and the "frequency" of message exposure can also be accrued from several different media.

9.2   PART II

9.2.1   Building Brand Image

The second phase of building media brand equity is to enhance the image or brand associations surrounding a media product. Whereas awareness addresses how well a brand name or symbol is recalled or recognized, brand image deals with the meaning or reputation of the brand. We will see that many strategies for image building are similar to those offered in the "Building Brand Awareness" section. However, awareness and image are not synonymous branding concepts.

A serious problem can arise when a well-recognized brand lacks any worthwhile imagery. Most American consumers today are probably aware of the corporate name and logos of Kmart, Wal-Mart, and Target, but when asked what each brand stands for or how each brand is different than the others in terms of consumer benefits or reputation, there can be some confusion. Similarly, some broadcast brand names can be recognized readily by most people, such as the CBS eye or the NBC peacock, but when asked about each network's image, many viewers will struggle for answers. These brands are recognized but offer little coherent imagery.

On a local market level, three competing newscasts may have distinctive names, logos, music beds, and sets, but the typical news viewer may be hard pressed to differentiate these competitors in terms of cogent thoughts and feelings about the brands.

9.2.2   Relevancy Builds Brand Image

At the very beginning of this book, we stated that successful brand marketing takes the consumer's perspective and dwells on consumer benefits rather than product attributes. Hundreds of research studies in human communication reinforce the idea that people will be more attentive and will remember more about a message if the message is perceived as relevant to their personal lives. Savvy brand managers know that some benefits associated with a brand may be more relevant than others. For instance, a car buyer may claim that gas mileage is one of several relevant factors to consider, but mileage may pale in importance when it comes to other factors such as safety, comfort, and prestige. A similar media situation could exist whereby a target viewer asserts that the quantity of local sports coverage is a relevant factor in choosing a newscast, but in terms of relative importance, the quality of the weather forecast far outweighs any contributions from the sports segment.

9.2.3   Emotion Builds Brand Image

Here's a quick branding exercise. Ask a group of people to write down the three most "memorable moments in their lives." Write their responses on a blackboard or oversized notepad so everyone can see the results. Now ask the group to determine what all of the responses have in common. After much deliberation and consternation, somebody's eyes will light up and they will shout, "They're all highly emotional!"

The lesson? No matter what the message, people will remember it better if there is a strong emotion associated with it. Brand managers can take advantage of emotion in two ways. First, they may use emotion in their advertising efforts as a creative tool to attract and hold a target audience. We have all seen how humor is a common (and award-winning) emotion in advertising. The second and more valuable way of capitalizing on emotion is to create an emotional benefit from using the product. Let's examine an example.

Seldom does Nike mention the functional value of its sneakers. Rarely if ever has there been an advertisement that concentrated on the design attributes of its shoes or the rational benefits of wearing them. Instead, Nike takes a more emotional road and talks about attitudes: "Just do it." Nike's image is about winning and all the emotions associated with a winner. In a world in which the functional benefits of most brands are more similar than they are different, adding emotional components to a brand image is a smart strategy. Although on a functional level a competitor may improve his or her product to be identical with your brand, it is much harder for that same competitor to steal away your brand's emotional imagery. Just ask Reebok.

Broadcast brands can apply easily the same emotion-based strategies. Unlike toothpaste or car mufflers, television "products" are usually packed with emotion, and indeed, the most important viewer benefit may be an emotional one. Even supposedly "factual" news programming can offer an emotional payoff for the viewer. The pacing, story selection, and personalities of the anchors can contribute to key emotional dimensions of a program. When attempting to enrich the reputation of a media brand, emotion can be a valuable persuasion tool. When creating a promo or advertising campaign, the brand manager determines not only what the target audience should think but also what they should feel.

9.2.4   Consistency Builds Brand Image

A message should be consistent across media and over time. Saying one thing in print and another in radio is bad branding across media. Similarly, saying one thing in June and another in July is also bad branding across time. All key managers in a business must agree on a compelling and sustainable marketing message that will not become obsolete in a few months. This message should be translated easily into different media configurations so that an integrated marketing campaign (IMC) can be implemented.

The underlying theory of any integrated campaign is that the whole is larger than the sum of its individual parts. By taking a more holistic approach, the individual media messages interact with each other, so that the overall branding impact is greater than the impact of any single media message. The "Just do it" slogan for Nike is recognized by many consumers, but they seldom attribute this recognition to any specific advertising medium. Instead, consumers claim that they hear and see it "everywhere." From television commercials and magazine ads to stadium banners and players' uniforms, Nike branding activities are completely integrated.

This two-fold strategy of consistency and integration can be applied to television brands as well. Branding tools such as *TV Guide* ads, on-air promos, radio commercials, bumper stickers, and key chains should exhibit a synergy in which the marketing message is consistent and uniform. Experts in integrated marketing often use the concept of "a single voice" to explain the necessity of saying the same thing through different channels of communication.

9.2.5   Simplicity Builds Brand Image

The notion of simplicity can be misleading. There can be a connotation that simplicity means small or superficial, but this is not the case. A more sophisticated view of simplicity can be borrowed from science in which *parsimony* is a goal in explaining very complicated things. A parsimonious explanation is one that explains the broadest concepts while using the fewest elements. Einstein's genius was revealed when he came up with the "simple" equation $E = mc^2$ to explain how the universe works.

Ordinary people do not want to be overwhelmed with information, especially information that seems disorganized or randomly assembled. This does not mean that the brand manager is stuck with only one message. On the contrary, a brand "message" can be plural, providing that each individual message is somehow connected logically to all the others. This unified approach to brand message making allows a business to say many things to a consumer. For example, a car manufacturer wishing to brag about several engineering breakthroughs can merge these elements under a parsimonious heading of safety. The consumer can then "attach" these many and varied brand associations to a few all-inclusive locations in memory. These locations are important to a brand manager as we will see in the next image building category: positioning.

A television example would be the marketing of a local newscast that has several strong, favorable, and unique brand associations such as

- A reputation for regional coverage using several distant community news bureaus
- An impressive fleet of newsgathering hardware, including live microwave trucks and a helicopter
- The most on-street reporters in the market

So how do we attach these dimensions into a simple yet memorable marketing statement? How about "*Eyewitness News* Is Everywhere" as a slogan?

Obviously, this type of branding exercise is a good way to create slogans.

9.2.6   Proper Positioning Builds Brand Image

As mentioned earlier, positioning is the process of defining a brand in relationship to its direct competitors. Positioning results in brand differentiation. The criteria for positioning can be both rational and emotional, but the essential guideline is that positioning is derived from the consumer's perspective. For certain obvious tangible factors, an intelligent guess about what your customers think may suffice, but as your positioning exercise becomes more sophisticated, there will be a need for in-depth audience research. From an electronic media perspective, a network, program, or even a feature of a program can be positioned according to a number of audience-centered dimensions. The strength of a person's response on each dimension can be measured using a five-point "agree/disagree" scale. The statistical results can be averaged and then plotted on a grid or "perceptual map." Finally, the relative locations of your data points can be compared. From this analysis a media brand manager can determine areas in which the brand is perceived as strong, positive, and unique.

For most business situations, branding is about being different, but there can be circumstances in which the goal is to be perceived as the same. "Knock-off" brands want to be positioned as close as possible to a vulnerable incumbent brand.

9.2.7   Primacy: Being First Builds Brand Image

As in most human encounters, the first impressions of a brand are often crucial to building brand image. Being the first brand to introduce a new product—even a media product—is a valuable branding asset. The fact that there is no competition, even for a short time, can have a long-lasting positive effect on a brand. Being first implies that the people behind the brand must be special. Qualities such as intelligence, aggressiveness, perseverance, and innovation come to mind. Consumers like to be associated with winners, and therefore, one of the most effective ways of enhancing a brand image is to portray it as continually crossing an imaginary finish line in first place: first with Doppler radar, first with the inside scoop on a political scandal, first on the scene of a train wreck, first with election results, first with tonight's lottery numbers.

There can be a downside to first impressions. If the initial brand associations are negative, it is often impossible to change people's minds. The durability of initial brand impressions can be a blessing or a curse. The adage of "do it right the first time" could not be truer for a brand manager.

9.2.8 Borrowing an Established Brand Name Builds Image

This strategy proclaims that if you can't be first, then borrow the equity from a brand that already has a positive reputation. It is no secret that well-known and well-regarded brands can extend their equity into new products. As presented earlier, this process has often been referred to as brand extension. Rather than support an array of individual brands, many companies, including media conglomerates, are shifting toward greater use of corporate branding, attempting to bring all products and services under a unifying mega brand. The challenge is to extend these brand images to the new product without harming the integrity of the originating brand.

9.3 PART III

9.3.1 The Key Is Concentration of Force

Although each of the above awareness and image strategies provides its own special ingredients for generating media brand equity, they all have a common denominator. Look back to the some of the vocabulary used in this strategy section:

- Frequency
- Relevance
- Simplicity
- Consistency
- Integration
- Positioning
- Primacy
- Extension

A singular theme that runs through all of these concepts is *concentration* of force.

Whether one is studying physics, military history, or broadcast marketing, there is a universal theory that to make a significant impact when applying a force it is not only a matter of how much but it is also of intensity. Which will have the greatest impact on your head? Getting hit by a 3-pound pillow or a 3-pound rock? The lesson for media brand managers is this: Don't squander your branding assets in a dozen different directions. Instead, concentrate your efforts for maximum audience impact. This means exploiting your promotion and branding tools to the maximum. From copywriting and graphics to postproduction and media planning, the guiding principle should be concentration. As with our earlier discussion of the notion of simplicity, the objective is not necessarily the reduction of marketing weapons but rather the coordinated use of these weapons to strike a singular blow to an opponent. Think of branding activities as a high-powered laser. The more concentrated the light beam, the more likely it will penetrate a target.

The history of brand marketing is filled with tragedies in which millions of dollars were invested in a branding effort that delivered no positive results. Admittedly, sometimes the problem was an awful product, but often the culprit was a poorly executed marketing campaign in which targeting gave way to tonnage. Many of these losing efforts relied on the theory that an overwhelming amount of advertising and public relations can achieve most marketing objectives, that the sheer weight of the effort is reason enough for success. But if this weight is delivered in an overly broad, disjointed manner, there can be a disappointing return on investment.

For every branding failure, we can find a David and Goliath success story in which a company with limited financial resources implements a perfectly conceived and executed marketing plan. Its branding messages "punch through" all the clutter and ambiguity of its competition and resonate with the needs and desires of a target consumer. Every shot fired is on target.

9.4   PART IV

9.4.1   Appreciate Your Loyal Customers

In addition to seeking new audiences and new advertisers, brand building also means reminding your current customers how much you appreciate them. It is far more difficult to win a new customer than to retain a loyal one. Brand awareness and brand imagery strategies should not ignore brand loyalists. Reinforcing their commitment to your brand is a simple matter of reassuring them that they made the right decision. This can be accomplished through advertising but also through special considerations for regular customers. A media example might be a television station that airs certain news promos inside its own newscasts, obviously not to draw new audiences but rather to remind the current audience of how smart they are for choosing this particular program. In addition, many television stations have generated large databases of viewers that have called, written, or e-mailed the station. This information can be translated into personalized direct marketing campaigns, in which the interaction between a loyal audience and its appreciative station is enhanced. Saying thank you can be a simple yet powerful branding tactic.

9.5 PART V

9.5.1 Managing Change

A successful media brand must change with the times without losing its connection to its loyal audiences. Customers expect and appreciate innovative change.

For example, Chevrolet made good cars 20 years ago, but automotive technology has advanced so much that today's Chevy is even better. Similarly, Sears has been servicing customers since the turn of the century, but its product lines have changed radically. Consumers are no longer interested in purchasing butter churns and straw hats, but a century later people still depend on the Sears brand for thousands of contemporary retail items. For a television news operation, the introduction of technology that helps predict threatening weather should be perceived as a welcome change. The lesson here for successful established brands is that necessary change should be perceived as *evolutionary* and not revolutionary. However, change for the sake of change can cause problems. Although the broadcaster may be tired of doing some things the "same old way" for years, the audience may find these elements reassuring. Brand managers must be sensitive to the important intangibles of the brand—recall our discussion of the need for enlightened corporate culture—its familiar core values and intrinsic meanings for its regular customers. Perhaps, the single concept of reputation is the most crucial brand factor in deciding to make a change.

When market shares slip and there is an obvious need to change the images surrounding a brand, it is important to assess how current brand loyalists will react to the change. In a desperate effort to recruit new audiences, an established brand runs the risk of alienating the few loyalists it already has. In brand management, change can be a tricky challenge.

9.5.2   Switching Brands

Change can come in the guise of switching brands. Media brand building often means winning the hearts and minds of audiences and advertisers that have an entrenched and often emotionally charged relationship with a competing brand. What is your immediate response when your alma mater fails to win the big game?—Bad referees, injuries, dumb luck. Was the opposing team just better? Of course not! The branding variables of stubborn pride and self-esteem must be addressed when attempting to persuade people to change their minds.

In general, people seldom change their minds about anything. Social psychologists talk about *attitude persistence*, which is simply a polite way of saying that people are stubborn. A well-entrenched attitude about a person, a consumer product, or a television program is extremely difficult to change. Dozens of studies have found that, even in the face of seemingly overwhelming contrary evidence, people will hold on to their original attitudes. New contrary evidence is interpreted and distorted to match their old preconceived ideas. We are all guilty to some degree of this rationalization process. Furthermore, most people are creatures of habit so that recurring behavior, such as choosing a daily television newscast, becomes almost mindless.

Most brand mangers don't have the luxury of working for a prosperous incumbent brand. Instead they work for the challenger; the brand that, in order to survive, must take consumers away from the incumbent. In this unenviable situation, changing consumer attitudes becomes the top marketing priority.

Often, the reason why a new brand is introduced is that research indicates that the incumbent is vulnerable to attack. That is, its high share of market disguises poor brand equity. The marriage between the established brand and its consumer base may be more one of convenience rather than true love. Good research can reveal vulnerabilities in competing brands and your own. As part of a strategic planning process, many companies conduct a standard SWOT analysis (strengths, weaknesses, opportunities, and threats) to assess the overall marketing landscape.

This information can be extremely valuable for brand management because the owners of a brand often don't know the true reasons why people like a brand. Television is no exception. Misguided tinkering with a struggling program results often in the program getting worse rather than better. As the saying goes, "knowledge is power," and intimate knowledge of the vital inner workings of a successful or failing brand can give a media brand manager the power to build, sustain, or steal brand equity.

If new audiences must be captured from your competition, these audiences first must perceive obvious and important differences between media brands. Going back to our three-pronged model of strong, favorable, and unique brand associations, we can see that two out of three is not good enough to motivate a brand switch. Even when the challenger brand generates strong, favorable associations, it still must be seen as significantly unique. Otherwise, habit will continue to dominate audience behavior, giving the incumbent the advantage.

If there is no established incumbent, television executives may face what some marketing researchers call "the curse of brand promiscuity," in which audiences cannot differentiate one brand from another in terms of added value. This leads to a heavy reliance on short-term promotional hype that has no lasting influence on audience behavior.

Realizing that familiarity is a valuable asset; a successful incumbent brand must effect evolutionary change that is consistent with its past. Challenger brands, on the other hand, must effect revolutionary change by appearing conspicuously different. They must overcome familiarity with a promise that is irresistible.

10 | Measuring TV Brand Equity

CHAPTER

Now that we have looked at the various strategies to build television brand equity, we need to examine ways to measure and evaluate our work. In the branding game, it is unwise to simply guess what is going on in the minds of audiences and advertisers. Brand managers can become too close to their product and lose objectivity (just as proud parents refuse to believe that their child is just an *ordinary* kid). A better way to learn about the real needs, desires, and attitudes of an audience is to invest in well-designed audience research.

Rather than commissioning custom research to measure brand equity, a broadcaster may already have many of the necessary research tools to do a good equity assessment. The trick is to extract the right data from these existing studies. The first part of this chapter begins with an overview of some of the major factors that can hurt or help the accuracy of a brand research study. It is called "Garbage In, Garbage Out," implying that what you get out of a research study is only as good as what you put in. The second part proposes various ways to measure television brand equity, including the use of Nielsen ratings.

10.1   PART I

10.1.1   GI/GO: Garbage In, Garbage Out

The consequences of poorly conducted research can be worse than the consequences of no research at all. Some brand managers become the gullible victims of bad science and therefore make bad business decisions. The GI/GO adage is appropriate for both consumer and audience research in that poor research procedures can lead to false or misleading results. The upcoming portion of this chapter examines briefly some of the research pitfalls that must be avoided.

10.1.2   The Attitude Versus Behavior Debate: What do You Want to Measure?

What people say does not always correspond to what they do. Although the ingredients of brand equity (awareness and images) reside ultimately in the mind of the consumer, straight "attitudinal" surveys are notoriously unreliable. Many brand researchers prefer indirect "behavioral" surveys because so many attitude studies have proven to be disappointing predictors of customer behavior in the marketplace. (If we believed many attitude surveys about television, we would be convinced that most Americans want to view documentaries and *Masterpiece Theater* on PBS. However, Nielsen surveys of actual tuning behavior tell a different story.)

Consumer behavior can offer circumstantial evidence of underlying audience attitudes. Let's use an example of head-to-head late evening newscasts, for which each night of the week there is a different lead-in program. A researcher discovers that for one station, there is a strong correlation between the ratings of a particular newscast and the ratings of its lead-in; the bigger the lead-in audience, the bigger the newscast's audience and vice versa. In other words, the program's ratings performance seems to depend heavily on its lead-in. Without asking people's attitudes, the researcher could conclude that this viewer behavior reveals circumstantial evidence of poor brand equity.

A research study that dwells too much on highly abstract psychological concepts is headed for trouble. The best advice for creating attitudes questions for a survey is to have some reference to a behavior. For example, instead of asking, "What do you consider important news?," ask "When you choose to watch a local newscast, what type of news stories are you looking for?" The second question has a behavioral component (choosing to watch) that may offer more reliable results.

10.1.3   Bad Samples Produce Bad Data

Because it is impossible to survey everyone in the population, we are forced to acquire a representative sample of the desired population. Overzealous brand managers are sometimes reluctant to admit that the most insightful questions, coupled with the most sophisticated statistical analyses, are still worthless if the sample is biased. A biased sample is one in which certain persons within the population have a greater likelihood of being selected than do others. When dealing with sample-based audience research, a well-designed random sample is essential. Otherwise, a broadcaster cannot project confidently the research findings to the larger population.

Along these same lines, the most abused form of audience research is the focus group. Originally designed to be a device for generating ideas, television executives have mutated focus groups into what they believe is a shortcut substitute for a survey. Instead of going through the necessary steps of creating a large, randomly designed sample base, the manager sidesteps these requirements by inviting a dozen people to sit around a table and chat about the station's programming. The consequences of this unscientific approach to audience research can be management decisions based on unreliable data.

Focus groups can help generate ideas, perspectives, and insights. But these smaller group gatherings should never be considered a reliable quantitative survey of the general population. In the proper setting, focus groups can be very useful in creating appropriate questions and hypotheses that will be used in a later survey.

Presuming the television broadcaster does elect to do a legitimate market survey by using a large random sample, there is still no guarantee that this sample is a perfect replica of the target population. As long as samples are used to represent a larger population—even perfectly random samples—the results will be estimates, not absolute measures.

Fortunately, this margin of error can be predicted mathematically. This margin will vary according to several factors, including the size of the sample and the variability of the answers provided. Professional researchers will use statistical jargon, such as standard error and confidence intervals, to gauge the probable error contained in a piece of data. These predictions are based on the laws of probability, which implies perfect randomness. If the study begins with a biased sample (i.e., one not random), these error calculations become meaningless. Broadcasters and media buyers often forget that even in the best of circumstances Nielsen and Arbitron ratings are filled with unavoidable sampling error.

10.1.4   Bad Questions Generate Bad Answers

Questionnaire design is a science unto itself. Here are just a handful of situations that researchers have found to be troublesome.

◆ The vocabulary and sentence structure of a question may cause a participant to provide different answers.
◆ The order in which questions are presented may influence the way a survey participant thinks about a question.
◆ In a multiple-choice format, the number and type of choices available can often force a participant to give a faulty response.

- A questionnaire may not allow participants to express how strongly they feel about a stated opinion, thus exaggerating the interpretation of the results. Similarly, many surveys do not allow the participant to say, "I don't know" to a question.

- A lack of anonymity or confidentiality may influence the credibility of a participant's answers.

- Revealing the identity of the company that is conducting the survey may distort a participant's evaluation of a brand.

These and a score of other design factors can result in wrong conclusions about the target population. An antidote for many questionnaire problems is to "test drive" the survey with a small group of articulate people who can provide candid feedback. This is a situation in which a focus group is the perfect venue for correcting a faulty questionnaire.

10.1.5   Bad Methodology Leads to Bad Results

The proper measurement of brand equity involves "leveling the playing field" so that certain marketing mix factors do not distort the diagnostic process. Just as holding a couple of barbells while standing on a bathroom scale will distort your true weight, so the manipulation of key marketing mix factors can obscure accurate measurement of your television brand equity. The methodology of a brand study must somehow eliminate or neutralize the effects of these troublesome variables. For television, factors such as signal coverage, audience availability, lead-in, counter-programming, and promotional hype must be identified and then controlled ("leveled") so that the true reputation of the brand name alone can be evaluated.

Let's borrow an example from the soft drink industry and the cola wars.

Suppose you managed the soft drink concession at a sports stadium. You strike an exclusivity deal with Go-Go Cola that no other cola beverage can be sold within the stadium. The day of the Big Game arrives and thousands of thirsty fans ask for Coke or Pepsi but must settle for Go-Go. This little known brand captures a whopping 100 percent share of the beverage "market"! But is Go-Go Cola truly the preferred brand?

Suppose you allowed the distribution of Coke and Pepsi at the stadium but retained control over pricing. For example, you price a can of Go-Go at 50 cents and Coke and Pepsi at one dollar. Thirsty fans would rather have Coke, but the pricing is so advantageous that they opt for the discounted Go-Go brand. At the end of the day, Go-Go's "market share" looks outstanding. But is Go-Go Cola truly the preferred brand?

Finally, you "level the playing field" by offering all three cola brands at the identical price. Now, measure Go-Go Cola's share performance! Only within this controlled or price neutralized marketing mix context can we evaluate properly the inherent brand equity among the three competitors. The sales of Go-Go Cola plummet. Television brands can face the same challenge when any artificial or contrived advantages must be purged from competitive performance measures. Television brands need to be evaluated in an environment in which marketing mix factors are "leveled" statistically so that the only decisive factors influencing viewer choice are the media brand names.

10.1.6   Bad Data Interpretation Leads to Bad Management Decisions

Let's presume an audience research study employs a good representative sample, a well-designed questionnaire, and a methodology that factors out unwanted variables. The final procedure is to analyze the results and make recommendations. Yet, even during this final step, there can be serious problems. First, there can be a statistical problem. Good quantitative analysis involves certain mathematical skills that may be beyond those of a typical brand manager. (We recommend a college-level night course in Statistics 101.) A second potential trouble area is in the interpretation and conclusions derived from the data analysis. That is, the mathematical calculations may be perfect, but there can be confusion as to what the numbers really mean.

The interpretation of statistical information can be a source of debate among managers. For example, many surveys generate statistical correlations in which two or more factors (variables) are analyzed to see how closely associated they are. A problem arises, however, when a close association is interpreted as *causation*. That is, one factor is presumed to cause the other to happen. Let's take an example from nature. There is a strong correlation between the time when the sun rises and the first cries of a rooster in the morning. However, nobody should conclude that the early morning crowing causes the sun to rise. Although this example might appear silly, there are similar situations in media research in which the silliness is not as easily recognizable. For instance, a high correlation between a newscast's ratings and the day of the week does not necessarily mean that audiences prefer the content of one night's newscast over another. The genuine cause of one night's exceptional ratings performance may be an unusual lead-in program or a "run-over" late start for a competing newscast.

Warning—Proof of a close association (correlation) between marketing factors does not necessarily prove causation. Only a controlled experiment can offer the proper insight concerning exact cause and effect relationships.

Another common problem in interpreting statistical results is the failure to recognize the statistical margin of error found in any sample-based research. Because small samples generate high sampling error, managers should not agonize over infinitesimal differences in comparative brand performance. This is particularly true with single-digit Nielsen ratings and shares. Nielsen provides some basic guidelines about applying standard error corrections to their estimates. (Yes, Nielsen admits to considerable sampling error in its own published reports.)

10.1.7   Recommended Quick Read

The National Association of Broadcasters (NAB) has published a short book entitled *Troubleshooting Audience Research: How to Avoid Problems with Design, Execution, and Interpretation*. Purposely written for broadcast executives who do not have a formal background in research methods but deal with research studies on a regular basis, this book provides simple warnings and recommendations.

10.1.8   Hire a Research Pro

The best solution to the GI/GO problem is to hire qualified professionals in the form of a reputable outside research firm or a properly trained in-house research manager. The consequences are too important to risk attempting do-it-yourself amateur brand research. As a cost-saving measure, many major group broadcasters have a corporate research staff that can assist individual stations. Regardless of who actually executes the research study, an astute television brand manager should understand thoroughly the basic principles guiding the measurement of media brand equity.

10.2   PART II

10.2.1   Ways to Measure TV Brand Equity

Earlier, we proposed a television equity model that consisted of two basic audience components: brand awareness and brand image. Now, we will take a brief look at several ways to measure these components.

10.2.2   Measuring TV Brand Awareness

Brand awareness relates to the likelihood that a brand will come to mind when given different types of clues. As mentioned earlier, brand awareness can be divided into recall and recognition components. We also discussed that in low-involvement purchase situations, top-of-mind awareness alone can drive brand choice.

For television broadcasters, this top-of-mind issue is critical for attracting occasional, or "soft core", viewers of program genres. For many consumer brands, the difference in market share between the first- and second-ranked product lies in each brand's capacity to lure infrequent users. For instance, a person may seldom watch a local newscast, but when he or she does desire some local news, the most familiar brand name will probably be chosen. From our discussion of "double jeopardy," we know that light users tend to be exceptionally loyal. Therefore, a highly familiar station or program can monopolize these infrequent users, translating them into rating points!

Measuring brand recall can be a relatively simple procedure. Survey participants can be asked to recall from memory the names of programs, features, talent, and promotional slogans. The order and elapsed time for recalling different competitive brands can reveal the degree of top-of-mind recall. Measuring brand recognition, or aided recall, involves the participants receiving some information they can trace back to memory. For instance, a person would be asked if they recognize any on-air talent from a list of names and photographs.

In addition to tabulating correct answers, recording *mistakes* in recall and recognition can also be a revealing research experience. For instance, if names, faces, slogans, or channels are attributed to the wrong program, the researcher can assume there is significant ambiguity and confusion in the branding marketplace. Which is worse? A brand that cannot be identified at all or a brand that is wrongly identified? Either case presents some serious branding challenges. Poor recall can be overcome usually by increased advertising and promo exposure. However, mistaken identity implies a positioning problem in which competing brands are not differentiated enough by audiences.

10.2.3   Measuring TV Brand Images

Once the competitive awareness of a media brand is assessed, we can move into the far more complex arena of brand images. As discussed earlier, brand images address associations that can be divided into the three measurement areas of strength, favorability, and uniqueness. Below are several ways these items can be posed to a survey participant. The first is an open-ended qualitative format in which the person essentially "fills in the blank" by using his or her own words:

Strength: What are the strongest associations—thoughts and feelings—you have toward the brand? What comes to mind first when you think of the brand name?

Favorability: What is good or bad about the brand? What do you like or dislike about the brand's performance? Does the brand stand for anything you care about? Would you call this brand one of your favorites?

Uniqueness: What makes the brand different from other competing brands? What features or characteristics does the brand have that others do not?

Remember that these brand associations can deal with emotional or intangible meanings, as well as the functional aspects of the product. For example, a participant may state that it is the warmth and friendliness of the television news anchors that makes one newscast truly unique among its competitors. Also, as a means of describing a unique branding factor, participants should be encouraged to talk about the intangible benefits derived from experiencing the brand. For instance, a viewer may feel more emotionally secure knowing that one station has a highly sophisticated piece of weather radar.

Rather than a qualitative open-ended format, a more structured approach would include a multiple-choice or what academics call a fixed alternative format coupled with numerical scales. This method fosters better statistical analysis of information than does the open-ended style of questioning. In addition, the participant can register the strength of the response. Table 10.1 is an example of a credibility evaluation of a television news program.

Unlike the open-ended questions, the results of this questionnaire can be analyzed by using statistics. Of course, in order to create such a multiple choice survey tool, the appropriate dimensions (brand associations) must be predetermined by the researcher. This may not be as easy as it seems. Focus groups can often provide help in coming up with possible brand association categories. Both qualitative and quantitative techniques have their place in branding research.

10.2.4   Measuring Relevancy and Importance

In a prior section we examined the issue of the relevancy and importance of image dimensions, concluding that in a purchase situation some factors are more important than others and that brand managers need to stay focused on those elements that will generate the most impact. There are several ways to incorporate this notion into an audience survey. A simple media example is shown in table 10.2.

Table 10-1. Newscast Credibility Survey

Please circle the number that represents how strongly you agree with the following words concerning the credibility of *Eyewitness News* on Channel 9 (5 = agree strongly; 1 = disagree strongly).

Impartial	Disagree	1	2	3	4	5	Agree
Accurate	Disagree	1	2	3	4	5	Agree
Trustworthy	Disagree	1	2	3	4	5	Agree
Factual	Disagree	1	2	3	4	5	Agree
Sensational	Disagree	1	2	3	4	5	Agree
Biased	Disagree	1	2	3	4	5	Agree
Confusing	Disagree	1	2	3	4	5	Agree
Irrelevant	Disagree	1	2	3	4	5	Agree

The results from this type of survey enable a television brand manager to have a sense of priorities. The results may not only indicate that the news set is not very good but also reveal that the set is not very important. Therefore, investing thousands of dollars in a new set may not be the most prudent branding strategy. A similar format can be used for sales promotion, whereby clients can be asked what elements of their relationship with a station are most important and how well the sales department performs on each dimension.

Another way to reveal these priorities is what we call a "take-away analysis," in which the survey participant is given a list of perhaps a dozen attributes and benefits that probably influence viewer choice. The take-away is an exercise in subtraction in which the participant must take away these items one by one based on how crucial they are for the brand's success. This process continues through several "rounds" until only a handful of priority characteristics remain that the participant considers the indivisible core of the brand. In other words: Take these items away and the brand's true audience value is lost.

Too often in a crisis situation, the station managers invest in expensive promotion efforts that have a minimal payoff ("Quick, build a new set, replace the music, hire on new anchor!"). These ranking and take-away procedures permit the brand manager to see the true essence of the brand and weed out those product features and consumer benefits that are not considered crucial by the consumer for the brand's survival. An abbreviated version of such an exercise is shown in Table 10.3.

Based on the above analysis, this station can not afford to lose its image dimensions involving weather coverage and anchor number three. These areas of the program are essential for its future success.

Table 10-2. Newscast Analysis

---

(1) To be answered before watching a newscast.

Using a five-point scale, please indicate how important each of the following items is in a newscast (1 = not important at all; 5 = extremely important).

The anchors	Not important	1	2	3	4	5	Important
Local news coverage	Not important	1	2	3	4	5	Important
The weather segment	Not important	1	2	3	4	5	Important
Sports scores	Not important	1	2	3	4	5	Important
The news set	Not important	1	2	3	4	5	Important

(2) To be answered after viewing a newscast.

Using the same topics from question one, now grade the newscast using a five-point scale. (5 = very good; 1 = very poor)

The anchors	Very Good	1	2	3	4	5	Very Poor
Local news coverage	Very Good	1	2	3	4	5	Very Poor
The weather segment	Very Good	1	2	3	4	5	Very Poor
Sports scores	Very Good	1	2	3	4	5	Very Poor
The news set	Very Good	1	2	3	4	5	Very Poor

10.2.5   Behavior-based Measures of TV Brand Image

The examples presented so far have emphasized attitudinal measures of equity, but we know that consumer behavior can also reveal circumstantial evidence of the strength, favorability, and uniqueness of certain brand associations. Information about the purchase, usage, and loyalty to a brand can be acquired from various sources. For the television industry, the most common measures of audience behavior are Nielsen ratings. Below are a number of ways to use Nielsen ratings to measure various aspects of television program brand equity.

10.2.6   Market Share

The most rudimentary way to assess audience strength is to "count heads." One can infer that in many cases the program or network that boasts the most people watching probably has a substantial number of brand loyalists. Earlier in our discussion of the double jeopardy effect, we found that the market leader tends to attract proportionately more loyalists than market losers.

Table 10-3. Take-Away Exercise

Round 1	Round 2	Round 3	Brand core
Storm radar	Storm radar	Storm radar	Storm radar
Bureaus			
Local news	Local news	Local news	
Weather segment	Weather segment	Weather segment	Weather segment
Sports segment			
First on scene	First on scene		
Anchor 1			
Anchor 2			
Anchor 3	Anchor 3	Anchor 3	Anchor 3
			etc.

Because of fluctuations in homes using television (HUT) and persons using television (PUT) levels, we recommend that share figures, rather than ratings or totals, be the primary unit of measure. Share is a better indicator of competitive performance on a "level playing field." For demographic analyses, which are normally not displayed as shares, this may require some calculations by the local management.

10.2.7   Stability over Time (Trending)

We have already ascertained that successful television brands tend to remain successful in that they deliver consistent audiences over time. Tracking Nielsen audience ratings over several sweep periods can offer evidence of the relative stability of a media brand.

10.2.8   Exclusive Viewing

Brand loyalty is the outcome of brand equity, meaning that a loyal consumer will exclusively use one brand. For a modest fee, Nielsen will extract exclusive viewing data from its diary or metered databases. This type of analysis is part of what Nielsen calls its Nielsen Station Index Plus (NSI Plus) client services.

10.2.9   Audience Turnover

Another indicator of audience loyalty is audience turnover, a calculation that incorporates cume ratings data. Cume is shorthand for "cumulative" and refers to the total number of unduplicated homes or people who watch a program over the course of a week. In other words, over several days a daily stripped program (such as a local newscast) will accumulate a weekly total audience that will be bigger than its daily average quarter hour (AQH) audience. For many years, radio stations have used Arbitron cume data to measure audience loyalty by dividing a program's weekly cume audience by its AQH audience. This fraction is known as a turnover ratio. Divide the fraction, and the result is a number called a turnover index. A low turnover (or low "churn") implies strong loyalty. Conversely, high turnover implies poor loyalty.

To date, television broadcasters rarely ask for cume audience information, so Nielsen has been reluctant to provide a great deal in its standard sweep reports. However, for a modest fee, Nielsen will generate additional cume and turnover statistics for a subscribing station.

10.2.10   Lead-In Analysis

We have already stated that taking advantage of a strong lead-in is a smart programming strategy, but the cursory results from these scheduling maneuvers should not be confused with brand equity. Television branding is about cultivating "appointment" programming, in which audiences are drawn to a program because of its content not its lead-in. Several research studies have confirmed that some television programs capitalize on their lead-in ratings better than do other programs. This occurrence can be analyzed from two points of view: audiences retained and audiences recruited. Audiences retained refers to the ability of a program to hold or retain its lead-in audience. Audiences recruited refers to a program's ability to attract or recruit audiences from competing channels. Programs exhibiting strong brand equity outperform their competitors on both measures.

In addition to examining the standard rating and share performance of two adjacent programs, Nielsen NSI Plus offers several types of "audience flow" studies that will track these two dimensions and present the results in terms of proportions as well as raw numbers. Program equity can be assessed more accurately by using the proportional data. For example, a program may have a weak lead-in, but the proportion of viewers it retains may be larger than that of a competitor. Similarly, the proportion of viewers recruited from other channels may also be considerable, again indicating an "appointment" audience.

10.2.11   Heavy Versus Light Users

From toothpaste and laundry soap to newspapers and television programs, dozens of consumer behavior studies have found that heavy users of a product category often behave differently than do light users. Although frequent purchases contribute mightily to a brand's overall market share, marketing professionals also know that heavy users tend to be less loyal. Conversely, occasional users tend to stick with one brand.

As a special request, known as a "qualifier," Nielsen can break out viewer behavior by usage. For example, a station may wish to look at viewers who watch local news at least four times a week and compare these data to a second audience group that watches no more than two newscasts per week. In many cases, a large portion of the heavy users tends to "shop around" among several brands. Also, the top-ranked station often attracts a disproportionately higher share of the light users. Because it is usually impossible to stimulate more usage of a product (Watch more news!), the next best strategy is to find more customers. Looking at the preferences of heavy verses light users of a media product, such as news, can reveal some interesting branding opportunities.

In addition to Nielsen Media Research, other companies such as Marshall Marketing and Scarborough Research conduct audience behavior studies for individual markets. These data can be used to enhance a broadcaster's understanding of target audience behavior and program brand equity.

10.3   PART III

10.3.1   Measuring the Competition

Although learning as much as possible about your own brand is indeed important, the art and science of branding is grounded in the notion of competition. Success (and your job security) is measured usually by how well your brand performs compared with the other guy's down the block. The following is a brief overview of a few ways competitive performance can be analyzed.

10.3.2   Indexing

Indexing is an effective way to understand quickly the competitive landscape. An index is simply a unit of data expressed as a percentage of a base score. The base score is given the index value of 100 and often represents the average score of all the data entries. Let's use IQ scores as an example. Informing a person of the number of correct answers on an intelligence test may be of little value without knowing how everyone else performed. Presenting the average score of the test group along with the individual test score may provide more insight, but if the goal is to determine quickly how well a person performed relative to the competition, a simple index is the better solution. An IQ of 120 means that that person scored 20 percent higher than the group average.

A television example of indexing would be a ratings analysis in which the base score (index of 100) becomes the average rating of all late evening newscasts in a market. The ratings of each competing newscast are compared to this base score and then converted into a proportion. Table 10.4 contains a simple example.

Rather than confounding the reader with a barrage of ratings data, the index scores give a quick evaluation of how competitive a brand is within the marketplace. In this case, Station A outperforms the market by 25 percent. Station B offers typical or average performance whereas Station C is struggling, achieving only 75 percent of the market average in ratings performance. This indexing operation becomes even more "user friendly" when a dozen or more demographic categories need to be analyzed among several competitors. A simple scan of an index column can provide a wealth of branding information.

Of course the market average does not have to be the only benchmark (statistical base). Instead, another standard could be used, such as the leading station. In the above case, Station A would be assigned an index of 100, and the other two stations' performance indices would be calculated against the leader rather than the total market.

Audience attitudes can also be indexed. Let's use a prior example of the News Credibility scales from earlier in this section. Here participants choose an answer between one and five. The next step for the researcher would be to calculate the average scores for all of the test phrases and then compare competing newscasts. As with our case with Nielsen ratings, the average score for all competitors could be given the benchmark index of 100. Now we have some quick competitive insight. A station may score high on a specific dimension, such as a 4.5 for "trustworthy," but reveal an index of only 110, indicating that on average all the newscasts in the market are regarded as highly trustworthy. Referring to our brand association framework of strong, favorable, and unique, we see that "trustworthiness" is strong but not necessarily unique, and therefore, the concept should not be the centerpiece of a branding campaign intended to differentiate brand competitors.

Indexing is also a handy tool for combining research results from different types of studies. For example, suppose a television brand manager wanted to compare Nielsen ratings data with audience attitude scales. The answer is indexing. By standardizing these data into indices, the results from all kinds of audi-

Table 10-4. Index by Ratings

Station	Household rating	Index
A	15	125
B	12	100
C	9	75
Combined AVG	12	100

ence studies can be incorporated in one presentation. A hypothetical example of one program in which (1) Nielsen household and demographic ratings (RT), (2) several five-point attitude scales, and (3) geographical coverage have been merged into one indexed presentation is covered in Table 10.5.

Comparing the original data creates an obvious "apples-to-oranges" (ratings to scales to populations) dilemma, but the indexing column resolves this mathematical problem and provides better insight into the program's competitive performance. Ranking these attitude indices top to bottom on the presentation would allow the reader to understand the relative importance of each brand characteristic. In addition, index scores can be translated easily into bar graphs in which the base index of 100 becomes the base line for the graph. Indices greater than 100 are placed above the line (+), while indices less than 100 are placed below the line. Figure 10.1 is an example of a graphic presentation of indexing.

10.3.3   Positioning

Recall that positioning deals with the proximity of a brand to its market competitors in terms of strength, favorability, and uniqueness. As with indexing, positioning exercises are designed to detect competitive advantages and usually make use of graphic displays in which the relative positions of competing brands are plotted on grids. Several grid layouts can be used, depending on the researcher's needs. Figure 10.2 is an example of one such grid using three stations positioned according to weather forecasts and sports coverage and a 10-point scale.

Positioning grids can accommodate easily indices as well as conventional data. Also, some high-end research companies may use sophisticated "multidimensional scaling" statistical software to reveal the "perceptual space" for different dimensions. Although the typical broadcaster would not be expected to be an expert on this type of complex analysis, he or she should understand the underlying theory and be able to talk intelligently with outside research firms.

Table 10-5. Index by Brand Dimension

Brand dimension	Raw data	Index
Nielsen households (RT)	17	120
Women 18–49 (RT)	8	130
Men 18–49 (RT)	10	75
Trustworthiness (1–5)	4.5	100
Compassion (1–5)	3.2	50
Impartial (1–5)	2	75
Population of counties reached (000)	65	100

Regardless of the level of sophistication, the essential concept of brand positioning remains fairly simple—it is the process of defining a brand relative to its competitors. The word positioning implies an observable location, a place on a psychological "map" where our brand resides.

10.3.4   "Blind" Experiments

The harsh reality for many consumer goods is that, in terms of actual product performance, consumers cannot distinguish important differences among competing brands. Marketing research literature is filled with examples of "blind" taste tests for soft drinks, beers, and cigarettes, revealing that when the brand labels are removed or rearranged, participants cannot tell the difference among brands. For example, one study found that the taste preferences between two leading soft drink brands varied radically depending on whether the test subjects were blindfolded or not. Medical researchers call this phenomenon a placebo effect, wherein a patient's expectations of performance do not correspond with reality.

Other consumer products, including some media products, can experience the same confusion. In many cases, what truly distinguishes one consumer brand from another is not its functional performance (such as taste) but the intangible brand associations or images attached to the brand names. This type of blind experiment can be applied to television. Here is one television news example:

Recruit a sample of typical local news viewers who claim to have a definite preference in newscasts. Make sure you have an equal number of loyalists for each station. Divide the group randomly into three test groups. Each test group is exposed to a hypothetical news story in which the only difference in the

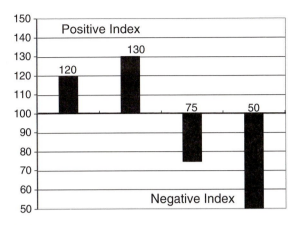

FIGURE   Indexing.
10-1

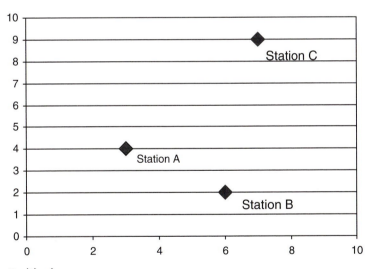

FIGURE   Positioning.
10-2

presentation is the channel and name of the newscast (e.g., Channel 9 *Eyewitness News*, Channel 6 *News Center Six*, and Channel 13 *Nightbeat*). The reporter must be a person that nobody would recognize (a "ringer").

After viewing the story, the test subjects were asked to fill out a questionnaire concerning the strength, favorability, and uniqueness of the news presentation. Brand equity researchers would predict that the true loyalists will be more generous in their evaluations when the news report is identified with their "preferred" newscast—even though the presentation content is identical in every other respect. This is the "added value" of brand equity.

Depending on the research needs of a station or network, different versions of the above experiment can be implemented. Perhaps sports, weather, and special features could be assessed in the same manner. The key to any "blind" experiment is to take away the brand name and see what happens.

II

The Practice of Branding TV

11 | Who's in Charge
of the Execution?

Thus far, this book has examined and explored branding and marketing in the theoretical sense. For the rest of this volume, we will point out some ways to turn theory into practice. The practical applications suggested were developed and honed in the trenches of day-to-day branding and marketing at stations that faced rating challenges. Although what follows is not necessarily a guaranteed road map to success, a thorough understanding of the daily challenges and opportunities faced by real-world television broadcasters will allow the reader to be that much ahead of the game.

11.1 WHO'S THE EXECUTIONER?

Many names are applied to the manager who is in charge of the station's branding and marketing efforts: Promotion Manager; Creative Services Director; Advertising & Marketing Director; Audience Development Director, and so on. For the purposes of this text, we will term this person the *Brand Manager*. We will also use the generic term *promotion* to represent any effort to market, advertise, or in some way apply branding to the station and its products.

We have also taken the liberty of including some basic information in the appendices for readers who may not have much experience in specialized areas. This information includes a list of recommended reading (Appendix A) and a basic primer (or refresher) on how to read a rating book (Appendix B).

Now, let us examine, in some detail, how the principles discussed in the first half of this book can be applied into practices. We will outline the basic responsibilities of the brand manager, evaluate the ways of communicating the brand message, and suggest a process whereby the principles can be implemented. As a way to realize how this process works in the real world, we will use a fictitious television station in a case study. Finally, we'll examine how to protect your brand in the era of intellectual property piracy.

And the future?

That's up to you.

First, You Need A Plan

It is impossible to know where you are going unless you know where you are. The best way to discover where you are is to research, research, and research. Specific research techniques are discussed extensively in Chapter 10, "Measuring TV Brand Equity."

A management team committed to moving its station forward will first make an exhaustive review of the following:

◆ The product
◆ The audience available for that product
◆ The sales potential for that product

A time-tested way of reviewing your plan is the SWOT method:

S = strengths
W = weaknesses
O = opportunities
T = threats

12.1   REVIEW THE PRODUCT

What is the product your station is providing? Is it news, entertainment, information, infomercials? Does it measure up to generally accepted standards? Is the technical end of it clean, crisp, and attractive, or is your signal fuzzy or hampered by geographic obstacles? Is your news coverage effective? Does it cover all the population centers in the station's designated market area (DMA) or metropolitan statistical area (MSA)?

When the results of this review are in, you should have a clear-cut list of your station's strengths and weaknesses.

◆ Do any of your strengths play off your competition's weaknesses?
◆ Do you have some weaknesses that are being claimed by your competition?

In both cases, you may have some opportunities to increase your strengths and diminish your weaknesses. Take a look at the following questions to lay the foundation for objectives:

◆ What are the major threats to doing this aspect of branding?
◆ How can you make any of these threats an opportunity?
◆ How are you perceived in the community as a brand?
◆ Are there "voids" in the market: areas in which neither you nor your competition is doing an effective job?

Answers to these questions form the basis of who you are as a station. And who you are as a station is your brand.

12.2   MAKE A LIST OF THE PRODUCT'S STRENGTHS AND WEAKNESSES

What threatens your objective of building on strengths and eliminating weaknesses? What potential opportunities exist or can be caused to exist? The wider you can cast your research net, the more likely your information will be close to reality. It does you no good if you just ask the management team. Go into the communities you serve and conduct anonymous research so your audience will not prejudice their answers either for or against you.

Every dollar spent on research early in the process will pay off 10-fold when the process is completed.

When the research and the management team has agreed about the station's strengths and weaknesses, more questions have to be asked. The answers to these questions will form the basis for your branding plan.

12.3   WHAT AUDIENCE IS AVAILABLE?

It is a fact of life in the 21st century that an information explosion is saturating the public's awareness. This is why it is vital to research the available audience and ask them what appeals to them. What would they change their current habits to look at? (If, for example, the available audience is predominantly over age 50, a younger-skewing product will most likely do a poor job in attracting or retaining viewers.)

Information on the life styles and habits of your audience may be gathered in your research and expanded upon in the focus groups. Knowing the demographic pod sizes in your audience will be invaluable when you place your media buys.

If you look up "Know Thyself" on a search engine, you will receive about 132,000 hits. But that venerable and much-used phrase is an excellent way to view your research. With the research questions answered, it's time to set the branding process in motion.

13 What to Brand: Setting Priorities

Brand managers live in a finite world of restricted budgets, limited manpower, and only 24 hours in a day. Although a typical television station will have a programming inventory of dozens of "brands," the true profit-generating business of broadcasting occurs usually among only a handful of these programs. People, money, promos, advertising, and public relations resources must be allocated according to some overriding guidelines. Priorities need to be established so that the brand manager's valuable resources are not squandered. Here is a series of recommendations for setting these priorities.

13.1 PROFIT POTENTIAL

Broadcasting is in the business of selling audiences to advertisers (and vice versa); therefore, any guideline must ultimately address the issue of profitability. Some programs and dayparts simply have more sales potential than others. The television brand manager needs to know what programs offer the best opportunities for the station to gain a profit.

For decades American retail businesses have used the "80/20" rule to manage their marketing resources. Typically, 80 percent of a store's sales revenue is derived from only 20 percent (or less) of all the products they sell. The same is true for branded television programs. Although a station is on the air 24 hours a day, the greatest sources of sales revenue are concentrated among only a few all-important time periods or programs such as Prime Access (7–8 PM eastern) Early Fringe (4–6 PM eastern), and Local Newscasts.

All key station managers must agree as to which programs should be considered top priority for station branding efforts.

13.2 DETERMINING SALES POTENTIAL

Several factors need to be weighed in this process. And, again, this process takes information from the sales and programming domains.

13.2.1   The Audiences Available to Watch

First is the available audience, or in ratings terms HUTs (homes using television) and PUTs (people using television). Winning isn't everything if HUT levels are too low. Earning a 50 share Sunday morning at 6:30 a.m. is a hollow victory.

13.2.2   Advertiser Needs

For many advertisers, some portions of the broadcast day are more attractive than others—regardless of the number of HUTs (HUT level). For example, the cost per thousand (CPM) rates for morning television tends to be disproportionately lower than rates for late afternoon or early fringe. In addition to the total number of homes, the demographics (gender and age segments) can be equally important. Sophisticated media buyers ignore total homes and focus more on key consumer demographics.

13.2.3   Selling "Demos"

A specific program may win its time period but remain a poor selling tool because of a disappointing skew in its demographics composition. Conventional wisdom holds that as a consumer ages, he or she is less likely to be swayed by advertising, despite having more disposable income. This is due largely to brand loyalty and attitude persistence. It is not age *per se* that affects this behavior. It is the fact that brands have become established over time. However, if a new type of product (such as cell phones or the iPod) comes to market, the boomers will shop just as younger people do. The problem is that so many ordinary consumer products (toothpaste, canned soups, car oil, soda, etc.) have been around for so long, "older" people become brand loyal and refuse to switch brands as readily.

Television is the same way. If a viewer has watched *60 Minutes* for the past 20+ years, they are less likely to shop around Sundays at 7:00 p.m. Rarely can marketing alter the demo composition of an established program. Conversely, a second- or third-ranked program may command high commercial rates because of its positive skew toward more attractive (or younger) demographics. These younger viewers are highly susceptible to channel grazing and need pinpoint marketing efforts to pique and sustain their interest.

When negotiating rates, media buyers will often calculate a target audience efficiency score for a program. They look at the time period's demographics to see if the message will reach more of their target demographic. If one spot will reach 10 percent more women aged 18 to 34 than does another spot, it gets a higher efficiency score.

13.2.4   Cash-Producing Avails

Another crucial factor for the brand manager to consider is the number of commercial opportunities (or spot pods). This is the number of usable commercial (and promotional) availabilities within the program. Regrettably, some sales departments look at the promotional spots as lost revenue rather than as opportunities to increase viewership.

Barter programs are often popular with station management because they don't require the station to lay out cash for a program. In exchange for this inexpensive programming, the syndicator retains a few minutes of commercial time for commercials it sells to national advertisers. Programs with a heavy syndicated barter commitment can steal away local avails, generating little cash flow. High ratings with high barter do not equal high revenue potential. In fact, syndicators of very popular programs to require cash plus the barter time. Network programs offer limited local avails. The majority of prime-time commercial opportunities belong to the network.

The networks also promote themselves using their own air. Because the nets want as much promotional support as they can get, they appeal to local affiliates with various co-op advertising schemes. Consider all co-op offers carefully. Beware of having either a network or a syndicator talk you into spending money ineffectively, even with a 50 percent refund incentive. At the very least have your co-op campaign tie in with your access programming or late news lead-in. Many stations are reevaluating their relationship with their networks, as well as vice versa.

13.2.5   What Will It Cost?

Stations invest millions of dollars in purchasing the syndicated broadcast rights for a daily program or local sports franchise. Operating a competitive local news department requires huge investments in production and talent. Group broadcasters invest in programs for distribution among their own stations. Each station has an equity investment in the future success of the program. The bottom line is that the company is looking for a return on its investment (ROI). Effective brand marketing strategies can help make these expectations come true.

13.2.6   Maintaining Audience Momentum

The branding game is a matter of both attracting and maintaining audiences. Maintaining audience momentum for a successful show should never be considered a low priority. Defending your number one position is vital to long-term success. Remember, successful consumer brands continue to market themselves to their current loyal customers. Media brands require the same strategy. Earlier we discussed the importance of telling your loyal audiences how smart they are for choosing your brand.

13.2.7   Lead That Horse to Water

Sampling is what marketing accomplishes best. The art and science of persuading audiences to break old viewing habits and try a new "product" is one of the cornerstones of effective marketing. This is no truer than during the time-honored annual television "Fall Premiere Season," when dozens of new programs need to be sampled. Some years ago, FOX challenged this tradition with their strategy of introducing new product throughout the summer months. However, there is a point of diminishing returns, because once a program has been sampled by a significant number of people, the continued success of the program will be dictated by the program content itself. Great promotion cannot resuscitate a bad program.

Notifying audiences of day or time schedule changes is also a priority. The smart brand manager won't give the competition an advantage by allowing some of your loyal audiences to get lost if their station's schedule suddenly and unexpectedly moves one of the audience's favorite programs! Many daily schedules at home are built around the viewer's favorite program.

Smart managers need to recognize lost causes: disappointing brand situations that cannot be rescued through marketing/promotion alone. For any branding effort to be successful, there is an assumption that the product is viable in the marketplace, meaning that there is some minimal level of consumer satisfaction associated with its use.

13.2.8   Something Special

Unfortunately, not every program situation can be categorized neatly into a particular level of priority. Locally produced specials, such as long-form news specials, may not generate a great deal of advertising for the station, but they often cultivate an image of quality and community involvement that can have positive impact on future audience ratings. The use of public relations and special events in branding becomes another tool for the savvy brand manager.

Brand managers may encounter the special issue of promotion agreements in which the station is contractually obligated to run a specific number of network or syndicated promos. There is often a tendency in the sales or traffic department to treat these spots as promotional inventory charged off against the marketing department's contract instead of cash spots. Be aware of this potential problem and how it may impact the on-air schedule for spots.

13.2.9   Dayparts and Image

The art and science of setting priorities is truly a juggling act. Remember that priorities are fluid. It is unlikely that current priorities will remain fixed for more than a few weeks. Things happen whether those that are expected and those that are unwelcome surprises—such as new competition in the market, declining viewership, or the defection of on-air talent.

13.2.10   Be Ready to Adapt and Change

In a perfect world, the brand manager would always project accurately what life will be like 12 months from now. But in the highly competitive, ever-changing real world of broadcasting, overly rigid, long-term projections are a straight-jacketed liability to good management.

Branding opportunities and threats will change inevitably and so must your marketing plans. Don't be blind to a new or unexpected opportunity. Keep your eye out for "sleepers": programs or features that initially held little promise but suddenly take off. Historically, sleepers have included such programs as *Star Trek* and *Friends*. Conversely, don't be trapped by lost causes, despite the pleadings from your network or some syndicators; you can't afford to squander your limited resources on battles you can't win.

13.2.11   Setting Objectives and Strategies

The first objective should be to either establish or firmly re-establish that brand. The classic example of effective media branding in the late 1980s and early 1990s was the establishment of the FOX network. Rupert Murdoch and Barry Diller faced the seemingly insurmountable task of taking on ABC, NBC, and CBS to form a fourth national network, something that had not been done since the days of the Dumont Television Network in the early 1950s. The savvy FOX marketing staff relied heavily on branding to position their product in the hearts and minds of America. They relied on branding so much that they invented new and improved ways of accomplishing it.

Crucial to this branding effort was the network's purchase of National Football League (NFL) television rights, taking them away from CBS. FOX became the football channel, the take-a-chance, in-your-face channel that had football. Football brought in male demographics and the opportunity to promote other programming to an audience that had formerly only been watching one of the Big Three. In the 4 years that CBS did not enjoy the audience brought in by the NFL, the venerable Tiffany network's brand lost awareness, especially among the younger demos and males, and their total audience shrank much more than their competition's total audience.

Other objectives, which follow branding, will be determined by the market make-up and situation. For the purposes of this book, we will confine our discussion to increasing brand awareness.

13.3   BRANDING IS NOT PROMOTION

As discussed earlier in this book, branding and promotion are not interchangeable. Although efforts to establish and grow a brand may involve promotion, much day-to-day promotion may not involve branding.

Promotion will be used extensively during the media sweep weeks to build and retain audience so the Nielsen numbers will give the sales department something to sell. Each February, May, and November rating period lasts 4 weeks. Most marketing departments add a week in advance of the start of the sweep, thus marking off 12 weeks of the year. In these 12 weeks, the station will primarily be concentrating on increasing the numbers of HUTs and PUTs tuned to their station. (For more details on ratings, see Appendix B, "Basic Training: How To Read A Rating Book.")

Promotion moves the viewer to use your product.
BUT
Branding moves your product into the viewers' minds.

The 40 other weeks of the year should contain a major element of branding as part of the station's branding and promotion mix. We will explore the ways a station can ensure this later in this book.

13.3.1   Set Timetables and Measurable Outcomes

Continuing with developing the station plan, you will need to determine realistic timetables to meet your objectives. Built into these timetables will be such variables as availability of talent and vendors, equipment delivery (if needed), any regulatory needs (such as Environmental Impact Studies), and any number of the thousands of other variables any business must deal with on a day-to-day basis.

By recalling that part of the goal is to move forward, setting measurable outcomes will allow the management team to know how they are measuring up against their expectations. These are way-points on your road map to success. Such goals may include the obvious:

◆ Increase gross sales (x%)

◆ Increase ratings and shares from sign-on to sign-off (x%)

◆ Increase late news rating and shares in women aged 18 to 49 (x%)

The goals may also include the less obvious:

◆ Increase fixed promotion inventory by eight spots per week

◆ Increase number of public appearances by anchors by five times per week

◆ Increase public relations efforts by three news releases per week

How are you doing with your goals?

Goals should be measurable and specific. And the plan must work toward the goals. Communicate these goals to everyone who can touch the product. Let the staff know what the station's goals are. Post them on the bulletin boards, in the newsroom, in the editing suites, and near the coffee machine. In the business lingo of today—get the staff all on the same page.

Now it is time to translate this plan into something that will gain the interest and attention of the target audience.

14 | Using On-Air Media for Branding

A television station's most valuable commodity is its own air. The brand manager has a tremendous responsibility to use this tool effectively to get the best results. However, in order for any good brand manager to know how to originate, build, or extend the brand, he or she must experience the brand. In other words, they must watch the program(s). Know what they are; know how and for what audience they're produced. In doing so, professionals must put themselves into the mind-set of their viewers. Their eyes and minds must not reflect the attitude of a journalism or broadcasting professional but must instead reflect the so-called average attitude of someone who makes their living outside the broadcast arena. They must discover (and research) these problems, attitudes, goals, and lifestyles of their potential audience.

14.1   NINE QUESTIONS TO ASK ABOUT YOUR PRODUCT'S VIABILITY

1. What is going on in the brains behind the eyeballs of the audience?
2. How will that affect the audience's perception of the product?
3. How can we appeal to those eyeballs with the station's product?
4. Is there a feature segment, such as a health report, that will appeal to the target demographic?
5. Aside from the obligatory news and weather reports, what potentially "brandable" elements exist in the proposed news program?
6. What inside the show will appeal to the brand's target audience?
7. What could drive away that target audience?
8. How can individual elements—the interstitials—be tailored to fit the branding message?
9. What elements can stand by themselves as a individual branding element?

All these questions (and more) must have accurate answers if the broadcaster is to do an effective job of branding the product.

14.2   PROMOTION SPOTS: TYPES, LENGTHS, AND WHERE TO SCHEDULE

One of the major keys to effective branding and promotion is knowing how and where to place those messages on the daily program log. Before we get more specific, let's cover a few basic terms.

Gross rating points (GRP) are a total of all the household rating points a spot will garner in a day, week, month, or any given period.

Fixed schedule is a contracted run assigned to a client (the marketing department). It is a contract you sign with your own station to run the station's promos. It guarantees placement in specific shows or in specific blocks of time, such as your afternoon or early news block. The contract provides fixed schedules for each program, for a contest, or for your entire promotion inventory. The products covered by this contract must be in concert with the mission statement. Your promo spot will be placed in a certain manner and won't be shunted aside for another spot. A fixed schedule spot is printed out automatically by the traffic computer.

Avail is a shorthand term for availability, an open or unsold spot on the log in which a spot can be scheduled.

Demos are demographics. What is the sex and age of the person who's watching?

Flow is the ability to move an audience from one show into the following show and beyond on your channel.

ROS is short for run of schedule, which allows the placement of spots on the log for a specific period of time (generally 5:00 a.m. to 1:00 a.m.), not necessarily in specific shows.

VOC is voice-over-credit-audio played at the end of a program over the credits. The VOC is an excellent promo opportunity to keep the audience from changing channels and to tell them about something specific, either the upcoming program, news headlines, or a contest.

14.3   DAILY GOALS

What do you want to achieve? Every marketing or promotion department has goals. So should a brand manager. Your daily goals should be a part of your overall goals, as discussed in the previous chapter. Be specific in what you want to achieve and what your priorities are. Your goals will hinge on your branding focus and your marketing plan.

Setting these goals will involve the general manager, sales manager, and program director, who will all agree on the program priority list. In other words, what shows get the most air time and marketing efforts, and in what order do the shows receive your attention? (See the previous section's references to the mission statement.)

Focus all efforts on these shows and dayparts. Make sure your whole department is on the same page. Then post the priorities. Posting this focus in your department is a good way to communicate and remind the busy creative people in the department.

Make a list of the spots that have required GRPs due to sales, syndication, or network requirements. Then sign a contract with the sales department for these spots to have a fixed position. The contract will ensure you hit the GRP levels. There will be several contracts all going at once to achieve all your promo goals. A fixed contract ensures correct placement on the log, ensures placement of your on-air work, and also keeps correct topical spots from running at the wrong days or times, an error that can be costly when positioning a new brand. This will also save you time on a daily basis.

Checking the log daily to make sure it's accurate and the spots are all running in positions needed is one of the most important jobs of the brand manager. Know the inventory of available spots. Keep a list of *all* spots, their numbers, their ending (or kill) dates, what type of spot it is, and, after checking with the station research expert, the demographic appeal of the spot.

Despite the widespread use of computerization in the traffic process, it is advisable to have a printout of the promo spot inventory. This printout will save you grief in the event of a computer problem. It also allows you to get a real feel for the daily flow of your on-air spots.

14.4   TYPES OF SPOTS

Daily topicals run the day of a program from midnight until the time it airs and is usually tagged "today," "tonight," "next," or "tomorrow". A topical has a short shelf life but is extremely effective. It alerts the viewer to a show that is coming up and will include an enticement for the viewer to watch it.

Daily topicals are particularly useful in news promotion. There is no other way to tell viewers what will be covered in the next upcoming newscast without a topical promo spot. These news topicals can be edited or done live from the news set.

Have a plan for promo replacement and have a plan for topical spot replacement. If you have newscasts, make sure that the news producers have a plan in place for promo preemptions in the event they need to extend their news time.

Expand on the plan. Make sure master control operators know the appropriate replacement spots in the event a topical needs to be pulled. Who determines this replacement and signs the log as such? Make sure the operators know where the replacements are located. Developing a good advance plan will save a major headache later. When determining replacement spots, always use a spot that underscores your overall branding plan.

A *date-specific* spot is an advancer, giving the date and time of a program in the future. It can be used for movie promos or a contest promo. Date-specific spots are usually logged no more than a week in advance and use a day and time tag, such as "Tuesday at 8." Advancers have a shelf life of a week or less.

Generic or image spots address the whole show or daypart in general. These spots are particularly useful in any branding effort. Generics have a longer shelf life and are excellent to use as plug-in spots for times when the scheduled promo can't run or for a topical that isn't produced for some reason. Keep them fresh! Generics need to be freshened, especially for shows that are no longer in production.

VOCs are little audio reminders that can be very powerful in keeping audience flow and, when cleverly written, keeping people from punching their remote control. VOCs are easy to write and produce in advance and can have enormous flexibility, including contest tinglers or news topical benefits.

14.5   BASIC SPOT INFORMATION

Most spots the brand manager will use are 30 seconds in length. However, other lengths will be needed for the broadcast day to be flawless: 20 seconds, 15 seconds, 10 seconds, animated logo "bugs," and the identification (ID) length of your network or traffic system—all will find a place on the log. The traffic department knows in advance whether or not specific lengths are going to be cropping up, so ask them at least weekly, particularly before writing and producing spots, if the lengths are going to be needed.

14.6   THE TRAFFIC COMPUTER

Traffic systems are highly computerized. They have to be. And, like all computers and software programs, each has strengths and weaknesses. The best way to deal with the traffic computer system is to learn it: not the specific programming commands, but the system's capabilities and limitations. Get to know the traffic manager and everyone who works for her or him. Ask if they can offer you "classes" so you can fully understand the system's workings. In the long run, it will help to understand the limits of the system. You won't expect the computer to do something it can't. The traffic staff can be the brand manager's new best friends with a little care and cultivation.

14.7   ASK QUESTIONS

Ask questions if you don't understand something about the computer system. Somebody will know the answer (and be happy to show you that they do). Just because it's a computer doesn't mean it's flawless. A check every now and then of the part of the system that handles the promos might save you an error on-air.

14.8   THE ART AND SCIENCE OF LOGGING

What spot goes where best? Placing the spot on the log to its best advantage requires a little thought.

The most expensive branding tool you have is your own on-air slots. The marketing and promotion department is the station's number one client, getting the most air time of any client. Time really is money in the television industry, and time should be viewed as such, particularly when placing spots on the log. When you're ready to actually do the log, you need to ask yourself questions such as: "Does it make sense to place this promo in this slot?" "*Why* is it appropriate?"

Spend time with the research expert to really develop an understanding of a specific time period's demographic appeal. Do you want to promote a relatively adult movie showing in a children's animated program? No, because there aren't matching demographics. Know the audience for each show and think about which of the shows you are promoting would be of interest to this demo. Write down each show's demo and keep it handy. Eventually, you'll know without looking, but have it written down when you begin. Match the demos or plug the promo into a spot that reaches the demo you want to attract.

14.9   IS THERE A BETTER WAY TO USE THIS SPOT?

For example, taking a 30-second spot and plugging a 20-second promo for your prime lineup and adding a 10-second spot for a news special report keyed to one of the prime programs is one way to effectively use the inventory.

Is this promo going to conflict with the content of the show you are putting the promo in? Talk shows need extra attention, owing to the varied and sometimes controversial nature of their topics. Viewers may object to a raw discussion of teen sexuality in the morning kid block.

Will this spot run up against a station ID that is promoting the same program or news story? A 30-second topical line-up followed by an ID is overkill and makes the station look unprofessional. The same thing can be said for entertainment spots. It is not effective to run a news ID immediately following a news 30-second spot.

Plug in the promos that are needed and that make sense, no matter what your own feelings are. And remember that just when you are sick and tired of seeing a spot, the audience is just beginning to catch on to it. So get behind it and log it.

Finally, remember two vital tips to make the on-air presentation effective and more professional. First thing each morning, right after coffee, check the log to make sure everything is in working order. This is especially true if you rely on overnight spot feeds or production tagging sessions for your fresh inventory. At the end of the day, before you head out the door, one more quick look-over will save you from wasting precious air time and will make the whole station look better.

15 | Effective Use of
CHAPTER | Advertising Media

In a television station, on-air is the first and most important medium at your disposal. But, you will use also the various outside (or external) media at your disposal to spread the branding message. Again, to ensure efficient use of the resources you have, you must be able to evaluate their effectiveness.

Use the Batten-McDowell Media Efficiency Profile (BMMEP) to determine how effective a given medium will be in terms of what to accomplish. This simple profiling procedure evaluates the media on these points:

- Geographic reach—How deeply into your marketplace does this medium reach?
- Demographic reach—How many of your target demographic does this medium touch?
- Frequency—How often will your target audience be exposed to a message in this medium?
- Change of message—How often and how quickly will you be able to change the copy or message with this medium?
- Copy capacity—How much of your message can the medium carry effectively?
- Emotional capacity—Can this medium communicate emotion effectively?
- Timing—Can your message get to your audience exactly when you want it to?

By using the profile, it is easy to see that each medium has its advantages and disadvantages. To evaluate them in terms of the branding goal you have, each of the above qualitative aspects is awarded a rating from 1 to 10, with 1 being least effective and 10 being most effective. (The BMMEP averages are rounded up for purposes of this discussion.)

15.1   THE MEDIA EVALUATION

15.1.1   TV On-Air

First and foremost, a television station must use its own air. It has all the advantages of the other media, with only one major disadvantage: Not all the right people are watching. The message is being shown largely to the station's loyalists.

Television's geographic reach is critical. A station suffering from signal problems or interference will labor under a continuing disadvantage, even in the world of high cable television (CATV) penetration. We will presume that, for purposes of this discussion, the station is on an equal signal strength with all the others in the market and give television on-air a geographic reach index of 8.

The demographic reach of television is subject to many of the same limitations discussed above. Again, for purposes of this discussion, the station is on an equal signal strength with all the others in the market and give television on-air a demographic reach index of 8.

In the perfect world, the brand manager would have an unlimited schedule on-air to propagate his branding messages to the audience. In the real world, the television station has to run commercial spots to pay the bills. The frequency of the message would be diminished by this real-world consideration to, at most, once per half hour. (Some forward-looking broadcasters carve out time in every commercial break leading up to the target program and schedule some sort of message for that program, even if the economics of the situation would normally dictate against such a move.) The frequency index for television on-air is 7. However, because the message can be changed quickly and easily, we will award the change of message index an 8 (presuming there are no production limitations).

The copy capacity for on-air is limited to the standard spot lengths (4 seconds, 10 seconds, 15 seconds, 20 seconds, 30 seconds, and—in rare cases—60 seconds.) It therefore becomes a challenge to the writer or producer to make the message effective within those time constraints. Copy capacity index for television on-air is 6.

Almost nothing communicates an emotion as does a picture. When the picture is wedded to strong copy and effective sound, it would have an emotional capacity index of 9.

Finally, on-air can be timed exactly. The television station owns the real estate where it is run and can carve that time period out for its own message. Television on-air has a potential timing index of 9. We note this is "potential" because revenue considerations may pre-empt the perfect timing slot for the message.

Summarizing the BMMEP index for television on-air

Geographic reach: 8

Demographic reach: 8

Frequency: 7

Change of message: 8

Copy capacity: 6

Emotional capacity: 9

Timing: 9

BMMEP average index: 8

How can the message get to those who do not watch your station's on-air? Simply carry the branding message on the market's other media.

15.1.2   Cable TV

The index for CATV will closely mirror television on-air, with the major exception of timing. The brand manager can only negotiate for the most desirable time slot and that slot is also being negotiated by the competition.

Cable's geographic and demographic reach will depend largely on the franchise areas available. In many markets, the designated market area's (DMA's) CATV systems have formed a commercial sharing network, sometimes called an Adnet. This network permits a single point of distribution to reach most of the systems in the market. In presuming this to be the case, we will give CATV a geographic and demographic reach index of 8, identical to television on-air.

Because CATV spots must be purchased, the brand manager is subjected to the limitations of frequency imposed by the available budget. These budgetary limitations balanced against the generally low cost per spot expenditures result in a relatively generous frequency index for CATV of 5.

CATV systems are upgrading their head end systems to permit more flexible commercial insertion abilities. Some systems have been limited by their equipment to a once-a-day or even once-a-week ability to change the copy. Because of this potential limitation, CATV receives a change of message index of 5.

CATV's copy capacity and emotional capacity are hypothetically identical to television on-air, which would award a copy capacity index of 6 and emotional capacity index of 9.

Finally, the timing index for CATV, subject to the possible limitations discussed in the first part of this section, is 5.

Summarizing the BMMEP index for CATV

Geographic reach: 8

Demographic reach: 8

Frequency: 5

Change of message: 5

Copy capacity: 6

Emotional capacity: 9

Timing: 5

BMMEP average index: 7

15.1.3   Radio On-Air

Radio on-air is a very effective medium for spreading the knowledge of the station brand message. How effective? Just listen to any popular local radio station during the next sweep and hear how many spots for television stations are aired (especially during afternoon drive time).

With radio, you have the advantage of being able to finely target the demographic group you want to increase. With an average reach in the demo of three at a frequency of 90 percent, your message should reach the audience. This results in a geographic reach index for radio of 7.

Radio's demographic reach for purposes of this discussion is also seven. The higher number than for television on-air reflects the fact that the message can reach the audience in their cars. In fact, that is preferable if the goal is to motivate the audience to do something (turn on the television to a given station) as soon as they make the afternoon commute home. It also reflects the fact that the competition's loyalists also hear the message.

Radio's frequency of exposure index is also 7. This number presumes the buyer has met the goal of achieving a demographic frequency of 90 percent.

The advertising message can be changed often, even hourly, which earns radio a change of message score of 9.

The copy capacity of radio is necessarily limited to either 60 or 30 seconds. Many radio markets sell a 30-second spot for the same price as a 60-second spot.

Most television stations break the 60 seconds into 30 seconds for a co-op syndi-cated spot and 30 seconds for their own product. (Some syndicators have strict rules as to how their co-op funds may be spent in this manner and a complicated reimbursement formula.) The copy capacity index for radio is 6.

The emotional capacity for radio is, of course, largely dependent on the copy and production values used in the spot. Before television's advent, radio kept millions of listeners entertained with powerful dramas (as well as the melodra-matic soap operas). The masterful comedian Stan Freberg is famous for con-structing powerful images in the theater of the mind. One of his most notable spots was produced for the National Association of Broadcasters (NAB) to promote the ability of radio to generate images in the minds of its listeners. (Think of a mountain of ice cream capped with whipped cream and topped with a cherry dropped by a bomber.) For this discussion, we will assume the message has been appropriately produced, and bestow an emotional capacity index of 8 for radio.

Finally, let us assess radio's timing. Theoretically, it would be possible to have a radio spot broadcast immediately before the start of the advertised television program. This theory becomes academic if there are six or seven television sta-tions all vying to be as close to the start of the 6:00 p.m. news as possible. However, because the ability is theoretically there, radio gets a timing index of 8.

Summarizing the BMMEP index for radio:

Geographic reach: 7

Demographic reach: 7

Frequency: 7

Change of message: 9

Copy capacity: 6

Emotional capacity: 8

Timing: 8

BMMEP average index: 7

15.1.4   Print

When considering print, the brand manager will be normally able to pick from several varieties, depending upon the size and sophistication of the market. Most markets have a daily newspaper, and most—if not all—of these daily publications will also include a weekly television supplement. Television supplements are also available as stand-alone publications (the most notable of these is *TV Guide*). Many markets have weekly newspapers; some of which may or may not include the alternative press. Finally, in this age of narrow-casting, there are more and more specialized publications catering to very specific audiences. Just look at the magazine rack in any of the major book chains and see publications for everything from cigar smoking to watch collecting to fountain pens.

Daily Newspapers

The daily newspaper will provide a highly variable geographic reach, depending on the make-up of the market. If the market has one major metropolitan center, the geographic reach will be excellent. However, if the marketplace consists of several medium- to small-sized towns and cities, the geographic reach will be defrayed by the cost of purchasing ad space in several overlapping publications. For the purposes of this discussion, we will assume that the market has one major metro center, which will give the daily newspaper a geographic reach index of 7.

The demographic reach of the daily newspaper tends to skew toward older and more affluent persons. (The best way to check this is to ask the publication for its research and compare the assessment of its demos with the targets needed to achieve a satisfactory penetration of the demo pod.) For the purposes of this discussion, we will assume the daily paper tends to be stronger in the 35 to 54 age group than in the younger 18 to 35 age pod. This results in a demographic reach index of 5.

The frequency of the daily newspaper tends to be much lower than other media, even allowing for pass-along reading (reading by people other than the person who first received the paper). Unless it is compelling enough to be torn out of the paper and posted on a bulletin board or refrigerator, the frequency will be one or two times per reader. This lower frequency will yield a frequency index of 1 for daily newspapers.

By definition, daily newspapers only allow a change of message once a day. This limitation will severely restrict topical advertising and will produce a change of message index of 3.

The copy capacity of daily newspapers is fairly high. Given enough money for the space (and an appealing print design), many ideas and messages can conceivably be communicated through the newspaper ad. There is, of course, a point of diminishing returns at which the amount of copy overwhelms the reader, resulting in either very poor or no communication of the concepts and branding message contained in the ad. The copy capacity index for daily newspapers is a substantial 8.

Likewise, the emotional capacity of the daily newspaper may be substantial with the right copy and design. Major advertising agencies love to fill a newspaper page with arresting graphics and snappy copy. Words and pictures can generate or capture emotion. The strength or weakness of the emotional capacity will rest squarely on the shoulders of the copy and graphics. Because this is so dependent on another force, we will award an index of 6 for emotional capacity.

Finally, consider timing. Can the message get to the audience exactly when you want it there? Unless the station is branding its morning show, morning newspapers would not provide the best timing. In the few markets with an afternoon daily paper, the timing for the early or late news would be more apropos. This lack of exact control over the delivery of the message earns a timing index of 4.

Summarizing the BMMEP index for daily newspapers

Geographic reach: 5

Demographic reach: 7

Frequency: 1

Change of message: 3

Copy capacity: 8

Emotional capacity: 6

Timing: 4

BMMEP average index: 5

TV Supplements

Television supplements would closely mirror the advantages and disadvantages of the daily newspaper except in three areas. However, because of the nature of the editorial product, the index would be raised by two points in frequency and timing. Both these areas would increase because the television supplement will be referred to time after time throughout the broadcast reach. Therefore, the message would potentially be delivered fairly close to the "point of sale" or the actual time a given program starts. On the other hand, change of message would be reduced by two points because of the timing nature of a weekly publication.

Summarizing the BMMEP index for television supplements

Geographic reach: 5

Demographic reach: 7

Frequency: 3

Change of message: 1

Copy capacity: 7

Emotional capacity: 6

Timing: 1

BMMEP average index: 5

Weekly Newspapers

Weekly newspapers would have the same disadvantage as the television supplement in the area of change of message because of the scheduling problems inherent in a weekly publication. It would also have a reduced index for timing because a weekly newspaper is less likely to serve as a television schedule. In cases in which a weekly publication has carved out this niche, the appropriate adjustment should be made in the index. The BMMEP index is a 4.

Summarizing the BMMEP index for weekly newspapers

Geographic reach: 5

Demographic reach: 7

Frequency: 1

Change of message: 1

Copy capacity: 7

Emotional capacity: 6

Timing: 1

BMMEP average index: 4

Specialized Publications

We won't attempt to build an index for specialized publications because there are so many variables. The interested reader may want to follow the line of reasoning for daily newspapers and make the appropriate assessments for the individual publications.

15.1.5   Outdoor/Transit

Our discussion of the advantages and disadvantages of outdoor and transit will make two assumptions:

◆ The market supports a healthy outdoor plant

◆ There is a viable public transportation system that permits advertising

Outdoor has a major appeal in our mobile society because either drivers or passengers will theoretically be exposed to the message it carries. Transit, either on the outer surfaces of transit buses or on interior cards of busses and subways, is primarily exposure to passengers and pedestrians. Outdoor is sold as showings. A 100 showing postulates that 100 percent of the potential audience driving on a given day in a given geographic region will be exposed to the message. There are also 50 showings, 25 showings, and specially tailored showings.

The geographic reach of outdoor is seldom as deep as the reach of a television station or even a radio station. Even in the most saturated of outdoor markets, there are places where outdoor displays are simply not permitted. For this reason, the geographic reach index of outdoor and transit is three. The same limitation would be true for the demographic reach index. The major exception to this limitation would be in the instance of a message that must appeal to predominately heavy metro or inner-city viewers.

The frequency index for outdoor and transit presumes the audience is in a space where it may be exposed to them. For this discussion, we will assume that up to one-half the available population is possibly able to be exposed to this medium. The frequency index for outdoor is 3.

Outdoor production is expensive, compared with the costs of producing messages for the other media. Unless special arrangements are made to "flag" a board with fresh paper every day, the medium's change of message index is 1.

An experienced outdoor/transit designer/copywriter will use as few words as possible to communicate a message. An inexperienced user will attempt to fill the relatively huge space with all kinds of messages and copy. Keeping in mind that the message must be read and understood in less than 5 seconds (the amount of time a typical driver can look away from the road), the copy capacity index for outdoor is 1.

The emotional capacity of outdoor is—as with all the other media—largely dependent on the ability of the copywriter or designer to pick the right words, colors, and images to communicate the message effectively. Some very emotional feelings can be communicated with two or three words. Therefore, we will give outdoor/transit an emotional capacity index of 5.

The timing index for outdoor is limited by the nature of the medium. Timing is not a strong point for outdoor. (One notable exception is in the outdoor-rich market of Los Angeles, where some enterprising stations and syndicators buy boards with messages that can be changed daily to promote the daily content of their talk shows.)

Many brand managers use outdoor and transit to support their major effort, not be the sole carrier of it. The timing index for outdoor is 1.

Summarizing the BMMEP index for outdoor/transit

Geographic reach: 3

Demographic reach: 3

Frequency: 3

Change of message: 1

Copy capacity: 1

Emotional capacity: 5

Timing: 1

BMMEP average index: 3

15.1.6   Online

You are, in effect, Spider-Person! You control your Web. Do you have the resources to make it work for you? The station's Web site is usually a joint function of news, sales, and marketing. The sales department uses it for value-added. The news department uses it to provide additional information and breaking news not worthy to interrupt programming. And you, the brand manager, make it hum with congruent marketing messages. Don't you?

The media index of your Web site is immeasurable, depending on the resources available to it. Because you normally do not buy it as one of your external advertising media, we will exclude it from this part of our discussion.

Now that we have discussed the relative merits of each of the media available, it is appropriate to look at how to purchase them.

15.2   NEGOTIATING RATES AND BUYING THE TIME

The growth of media buying services, some specifically targeting local television station needs, has been a real bonus for brand managers. The services handle volume and have special deals with group owners of radio and newspapers. Investigating how one of these services might aid your efforts is always a good idea, even if the station does not plan to use it. The sales department will be able to identify the active media buying services.

If you are buying on your own, call the business office and see how to set up an in-house agency name and tax identification number. This will enable the station to get a 15-percent discount, the amount accorded all full service agencies for client markup of airtime purchases. Now, you now already have 15 percent more to spend.

You must also familiarize yourself with two more media terms:

Cost per thousand, known as CPM, is the way agency buyers determine whether or not their clients are spending their ad dollars efficiently. CPM determines the cost of reaching a thousand people with this message. A $5,000 spot in a program with 5,000 viewers yields a CPM of $1,000. A $5,000 spot in a program with 50,000 viewers yields a CPM of $100.

Cost per point, known as CPP, is an alternative way of calculating advertising efficiency. The "point" in CPP is a specific demographic rating point. If you are selling laundry detergent, you would want to concentrate on demographic points in women aged 18 to 34 and would look at a CPP in that demo.

Before beginning, look at the available in-house resources. Will you have to provide outside media materials and finished products that will back up your department work flow? Is there money available in the budget for freelance or outside service contract work in the form of the following?

◆ Radio talent and distribution

◆ Print layout

◆ Billboard printing

◆ Messenger services

Will you have to shave those costs from the budget?

Once you have your full media budget set, it's time to use the BMMEP to determine how much of the budget will be divided between the following:

◆ CATV

◆ Radio

◆ Newspaper

◆ Outdoor

Call the sales manager and get a list of the cable and radio buys that are made on your station. This list will help you in several ways:

Your station already has a relationship with the media outlet.

Placing a buy, even a token buy, on these stations will sidestep possible (political) problems down the road for your sales department.

Call the person who is in charge of doing the station's research and ask them to pull a media list for you. It will include a report on all the stations in the market and their latest available ratings and formats. From this, you will be able to highlight the stations that fit your news demo. For purposes of this discussion, we will assume that demo is women aged 18 to 34.

Call the radio stations in the market and request a sales rep. Get them to set up an appointment to come talk to you; tell them you're thinking of placing a buy. Then do the same for the cable outlets in the market. Many markets have ad networks that feed all the cable outlets, which will make the calling easier.

This will some take time, but the time will be worth it. The point of the first meetings is to listen. You will learn how the stations see themselves and get brought up to date should any changes have occurred since you used your other media research.

Give each station a ballpark figure on the amount you might be spending and let them put together a proposal for you. Make sure they are aware you are looking for the best cost available and ask for value-added.

Value-added consists of the extra things a cable/radio outlet can do to enhance your message and, hence, keep your buy. These may range from adding your logo to the local weather channel updates to doing a major contest with the top radio station in town. This is how value-added stretches your dollars spent, and it stretches the message. Make sure the stations know you're looking to extend your dollars and you're looking for a way to put your four anchor people in the public eye.

Think like a public relations pro, combining the dollars spent with the value-added possibilities. If your market has a news/talk radio station, concentrate on them in a different vein. See if one of your anchor talents might become part of their programming, or book your anchors or reporters to be interviewed by the morning or afternoon drive hosts. It is vital to make sure you let the news director know about this possibility. News directors have very strong opinions about their talent's public appearances, and they also know what the talent contracts contain regarding these potential appearances.

Once you have all the proposals, write up a media purchase plan and submit it to the general manager with a copy to the sales manager. Let them know the buys you're about to make. Then ask each of the participants to sharpen their pencils. Media buying is a negotiation. It's not shopping retail. Act as if the prices are close to what you have but you need a little more shaved off so you can make your budget. This is an unpopular and sometimes uncomfortable aspect of media buying, but it can also be the aspect of it that gets you the best price per spot. It's usually done via phone. And be prepared to pledge the buy before you hang up. That's why you've already received a pre-approval from the general manager. Anything you save from this moment out will make you look good and can be used to cover production costs or additional, unexpected media.

Bargain, bargain, bargain. Everything is negotiable.

16

Public Relations and Contests as Branding Tools

Public Relations (PR) is another branding medium that can reach audiences who may not be strongly influenced by the more traditional forms of advertising. Human nature is such that an opinion expressed by a supposedly impartial third party (e.g., friend, neighbor, relative, reviewer) carries more weight in forming or reinforcing an opinion partially formed through advertising than does straight advertising. If a potential movie viewer sees advertising about a new movie, he or she may form their opinion as to whether they will be motivated to buy tickets for the movie based on the opinion by the movie reviewer on the network morning program or the opinion of a co-worker or neighbor.

Good PR may be free or very inexpensive, especially when compared to the costs of an advertising campaign to reach the same population. A positive story in the newspaper or a guest appearance on a radio talk show will get through to many more people than will advertising in the same media.

Why? Because positive PR comes across as an "editorial endorsement" of the person, item, or project. It is not necessarily filtered out by a consumer's subconscious advertising filters. The consumer thinks that positive PR is not controlled by an advertiser and therefore considers it a disinterested third party's opinion.

Good PR is often far more credible than advertising. A Broadway producer knows that he or she can buy a full-page ad in the *New York Times*. And so does the public. But the Broadway producer also knows that a positive review by the *New York Times* reviewer is a virtual guarantee of a long run. In our perfect world, a full-page ad would run across from the positive review.

Lack of control is the downside to PR. Just as a positive review will almost guarantee success for a Broadway show, a negative review will also almost always guarantee a quick closing. The realistic brand manager must acknowledge that it is impossible to manipulate every element of PR the way every element of advertising can be controlled.

PR can be used as an advertising and promotion tool, but not necessarily as a branding tool. The moment a supposed disinterested third party parrots an organization's branding statement, the average consumer will begin to sense that something is wrong with this supposedly disinterested third party. For example, suppose one of your important brand image dimensions is your station's association with a local sports franchise. Use PR to set up a visit to a local children's hospital with your sports anchor and some local team players. This should result in exposure from the local newspaper, hospital internal and external newsletters, and, of course, the station's own news coverage. This has a side benefit in that it may also give the news department an entré into the hospital when they need to talk to a medical source. One general manager is fond of saying, "If my station does something and we didn't cover it, then it didn't happen."

PR can also be used as damage control. The classic example of this is the unfortunate series of crimes involving tampered bottles of Tylenol. Tylenol's maker immediately set out to (1) acknowledge there was a problem; (2) recall ALL Tylenol products, even those brands not involved in the tampering; (3) explain the steps being taken to make the bottles tamper-proof; and (4) make the company's upper management available for any and all press exposure. Even though this course of action cost the company millions, the public perceived that Tylenol's maker was taking positive action on behalf of the public, and the brand came back stronger than ever.

PR plans are targeted to specific audiences. You'll be dealing with three distinct kinds of PR:

Outside PR targets the broad-based group of your station's viewers.

Business PR targets clients, potential clients, investors, and community and governmental leaders.

Internal PR targets station personnel to keep them informed about what's going on where they work: What the station is doing, when events are taking place, special employee efforts they should know about, and personnel changes and additions.

You have a range of media to use and know about with PR. Newspaper, radio, newsletters, special events magazines, and special events.

With all the options, what comes first?

Like taking a trip, know where you're headed. Ask yourself what you want to do. By identifying goals you will know exactly what you want to achieve. If you want a story about the station or a picture in a trade publication, you can make it happen.

16.1   THE MEDIA RELEASE

Media releases follow a fundamental form, giving news outlets a quick, easy-to-read information sheet that tells your story. This goes for the conventional, or paper, releases or for the electronic releases sent through the Internet.

All releases have the following:

◆ A headline

◆ A subhead—describing more detail about the story

◆ Date and city of origin of the news item

◆ Station contact name (for quotes)

◆ Station phone number, as well as fax and e-mail

Begin the release with a strong first sentence. Recall the journalistic W's: who, what, where, when, and why, as well as the additional how. If you have a question about how this format should look, ask some one in your newsroom for a copy of a recent press release, or get a network press release and copy that format. Failing either of those, hop on the Internet and search for "news release" (in quotes). You will probably get tens of thousands of examples.

Keep in mind your release is a direct representation of your station to the other media, so think before writing and make sure you have everything spelled correctly.

If you are sending a picture with the release, make sure it's the kind of picture that the publication needs. On the back of the picture, take a blank white sheet and put the name of the persons depicted, their titles, and what the picture is about. This sheet of paper is called a cut sheet. Fold the cut sheet over the bottom of the picture so the information shows on the front. Include the station contact and phone on the cut sheet, too. The same goes for a JPEG/JPG you include in an electronic press release.

You are in a creative business, so be creative with your press releases. Ask yourself: "How do I get attention?" and "How can I get attention with this news?" Perhaps a memorable leave-behind will back up the news you want to share.

16.2   CONTESTS

Contests also present opportunities to extend brand awareness. They garner attention from consumers who, true to human nature, are looking for something for nothing. If the prizes are appropriate to the brand, they may provide opportunities for brand sampling. This is especially true in broadcasting, in which contests are used extensively (and sometimes exclusively) to increase viewing for a sweep period.

There are a number of good reasons for stations to conduct contests. The first and most obvious is to drive viewership to targeted day-parts. For example, contests can be very effective in building viewership to early fringe or newscasts, and they create awareness of a new program or new programming line-up. They provide an opportunity for a station to affect viewing habits by forcing the audience to watch.

Contests are also used by many sales departments as a way of providing value-added aspects for clients. If a client can see increased traffic because of a contest, the sales department can press for a renewal at higher rates.

One unusual way contests can benefit your station is through database marketing. How? Because people who enter contests have demonstrated their willingness to be a part of a two-way communication. The reasoning goes that because they are willing to talk with the contest sponsor, they will be more likely to be a part of a ratings sample universe. If they cooperate with Nielsen, the reasoning goes, these responders may be influenced by the contesting station's efforts. Thus a database with people who have demonstrated a willingness to cooperate in responding to surveys may be built by the savvy contest sponsor and potentially used to influence Nielsen families directly.

Contests may be tailored to appeal to specific demographics. For example, if a station wishes to build its young male viewership, it will conduct a contest with prizes that appeal to young males. The same principle holds if a station wants to build viewership in fringe counties. It may use direct mail in those counties (in addition to contest piece distribution in other, more generalized outlets, such as a fast-food chain).

For example, again suppose one of your important branding associations revolves around a local team. It is easy to create a contest with a prize such as a set of season tickets. This contest not only drives viewership but also establishes a close brand association between the station and the team in the minds of audiences. This simple contest thereby positions your station against the competition that was too late to get on the ball!

The TV Station: WFXX

For the rest of this discussion about the practices of branding, we are going to apply the principles discussed to a mythical television station, which we have named WFXX. You may find more information here than you ever thought you would need, but we wanted to give you as many of the nuances of working in a "real" television station as possible.

17.1   WFXX

WFXX is the FOX television affiliate in a six-station medium-sized market (size 25 to 45) in the mid-Atlantic region of the United States. The designated market area (DMA) covers 14 counties, ranging from the heavily populated metropolitan counties to the sparsely populated rural counties in the southwest part of the market.

WFXX is about to begin a 10:00 p.m. newscast, having previously never done news in any form. In addition, it has been asked by the PAX affiliate in town to provide hourly prime-time headlines when the news operation starts up.

17.1.1   The Details

WFXX is channel 33.

It is owned by a large media corporation, which bought it from the family who signed the station on the air in the late 1960s as a primarily religious broadcaster.

The station's building is located in the downtown area of the city, but not in the hub of business or sports activity. The building is not a showplace.

The ownership is struggling with keeping the equipment up to par. In the past 6 months, a plan has been put in place to replace and upgrade equipment.

The chief engineer knows he has to get the plant ready to go digital, so everything will be capable of handling digital and high-definition television (HDTV) formats when the need arises. By the time the 10 o'clock news report signs on, the station will boast state-of-the-art technology to take it well into the new century. The HD transmitter will also be installed, and the sales department is lobbying for an all-infomercial stream of programs on the unused bandwidth.

The general manager was the general sales manager at the company's flagship station in a major market. This is her first time at the helm, and she is acutely aware of the pressures put on her by the corporation. She knows the value of marketing, branding, and promotion, but she still has to please her bosses with her monthly performance numbers. She also *likes* the idea of an all-infomercial channel.

The company has made a major commitment to put a newscast on the air. Their standard business model forecasts that it will not make money for the first two years, but the rest of the operation will have to compensate for any profit short-fall. That translates into smaller budgets for other departments.

The news department is being assembled, and the four main anchors consist of the following:

Anchor man–age 52 and graying, he has been in the market for a decade and is moving over from another station where he was being underutilized. His hire is somewhat of a coup because he had once been a major anchor at the NBC affiliate.

Anchor woman–age 34, pretty, moving into her first main anchoring job from the weekend slot in Albuquerque. She is married to stockbroker, who is moving with her. She also has a young daughter and a 1-year-old baby son.

The weather person–age 34, is very classy, has the American Meteorological Society (AMS) seal, was number 4 (weekends) for a large station in San Francisco and wants to be the star in his own right. He loves his gadgets and is willing to go out to speak to science classes 3 days a week, weather permitting.

Sports guy–age 29, single. Former baseball player who is not too bright, but affable. He had one season in the majors before injuries forced his retirement.

The news director is in his late 30s and has been a news director for seven years at medium market stations in Michigan, Nebraska, and Ohio. He is from this market, and he took the job because he wanted to return home. He feels promotion should be in his control and is somewhat suspicious of outside promotion plans, fearing they will compromise the credibility of his reporters. He has convinced the organization that the news must be called *WFXX Metro News*, to carve out a position in the viewers' minds. He likes the idea of having his talent on another station, which has led to a number of spirited discussions regarding how they will be branded.

The reporters are a mix from within the market of those who did not get their contracts renewed by the competition and new college graduates from the state university system's highly regarded school of journalism.

WFXX has had the call letters only two years. People in the market still refer to them as their old calls: WGDD (W-good).

17.2   THE COMPETITION

Our mythical market has an overabundance of competing media. They represent all the networks and weblets, and all compete to establish their own brand with the audience.

17.2.1   Channel 3

The number one news ratings station in the market is an 900-pound gorilla. It is an NBC affiliate with Oprah leading into the 5:00 p.m. *Action News*. Their local news block runs until 6:30, when the NBC network news starts. This is followed at 7:00 by two highly popular (but older skewing) syndicated programs. They also have a half hour at 11:00 and an early morning line-up of news from 5:00 a.m. until the start of the *Today Show*.

Their budgets are high, with new sets, updated graphics, and a very stable on-air group of anchors. But there is trouble in paradise for the first time in a long while. Their anchor lady is talking about leaving, and the rumors are that the new news director is a tyrant. They will deny it to their dying day, but the station initially rose to the top of the market by finding and exploiting "sensational" news stories. They now aspire to be "capital J" journalists.

17.2.2   Channel 7

The number two operation is a scrappy but classy station with a solid, no-nonsense approach to news. Their anchor man has been on the air for 30 years and is black. After a succession of news directors, they have settled on one who is closing in on a year at the station and has made positive changes. They lost their very popular weather person to marriage and a move out of town, and the replacement has not been very well received. They are not very sure about who they are on-air and have changed their look twice in the past year. They do the exact hours of news as Channel 3. A CBS affiliate, their demos are a slightly bit older, but they seem happy to use this as a base on which to build.

17.2.3   Channel 10

The ABC station is a trailing number three, but they are spunky. They will try anything to get numbers, including some ambulance chasing and seedy undercover reports on prostitution and strip clubs. Their general manager is a former news director from San Francisco, and this is his first time at the helm of a station. Their anchors are all young, pretty, and pretty much nondescript. They change positions like the wind and have recently been stung with some bad performances by their technical people, which has been written up in the newspaper.

17.2.4   Channel 24

A WB affiliate, with no news presence at all. They run *Law and Order* at 10:00 p.m., followed by *Seinfeld* at 11:00 p.m. against the other newscasts.

17.2.5   Channel 45

This is a PAX net station with updates read by a young intern reporter during their prime time. They seem to survive on paid programming and the ubiquitous *Touched by an Angel*. They figure to cash in on the cachet of news by using your news reporters during their hourly headline breaks.

17.3   THE MARKET ECONOMY

The major businesses in the market include government, two auto plants, headquarters to a major Baby Bell, a snack food manufacturer, and an oil refinery. There are two medium-sized universities and a large junior college specializing in technical training to feed the labor needs of the auto plants. There is a lot of shift work in the market, much of it working women. The switch to an on-line work place is slow to catch on, and picture cell phones are still considered yuppie. The people in the market are good people. Change is hard for them to deal with as they find their income level is falling while their age is increasing.

There is a ray of hope on the horizon in a new Mayo-type clinic, which, in conjunction with the large university medical school, is already bringing national and international notice.

The market has one morning daily newspaper with a popular television supplement, 23 different radio stations encompassing nine major formats (including two carrying National Public Radio, or NPR), a healthy outdoor and transit plant, and a variety of advertising driven weekly publications.

This is the complex and fascinating arena in which you have to work your marketing and branding magic.

17.4   BASIC BRAND POSITIONING GUIDELINES

As WFXX's brand manager, it falls to you to work with the team to come up with a positioning or branding statement for the highest impact on your audience. This statement will tell the audience who you are and what you stand for. Therefore, you should be familiar with some of the basic guidelines for a branding process as outlined in Section I of this book. Work with these ideas and concepts in developing and hammering home your brand positioning.

17.4.1   What's in It for Me?

Known as WIFM (pronounced whiff-em), this is the overwhelming concern of your audience. They must be able to know, appreciate, and embrace the benefit your position offers them. If you tout your Doppler radar, the audience must know how it will help them save their property and their lives. If you have the earliest newscast in the market, tell your viewers that you did it so they could get a head start on their world each day. If your news anchors are not from your market, let them tell your audience how much they love living there.

17.4.2   Is It Simple?

Make sure your chosen positioning statement is simple. *Parsimonious Wordsmithing* is the way to go. Say everything with very little effort. It must be easily understood and remembered. The statement must also be able to be incorporated into everything you and your station do. This synergistic requirement will come back to either bless you or haunt you unless you think it through.

17.4.3 Does It Hit Your Target Audience?

Your positioning dimensions must be important to your target audience. If your station has chosen the proverbial soccer mom as its target audience, ensure that your branding is reflected in your graphics, music, and on-air philosophy. Here is where some money spent in researching the wants and needs of your target audience will pay off in overwhelming dividends. Whatever you do, do not scrimp on research. You could end up like a famous clothing maker who ignored the research that said it should stick to its core product. Against the advice of researchers (and customers), it expanded into other lines and almost went bankrupt.

17.4.4 Does It Have Both Tangible and Intangible Aspects?

When selecting your positioning statement, it is important to be sure you have introduced some intangible positioning with it. The emotional or even irrational feelings your statement induces in the minds of the audience will make it much more difficult for your competitors to rip off and thereby steal your thunder. However, don't ignore the functional and rational positioning either. Being "the station where people cry a lot" contains emotion and is certainly not rational, but it has no concrete *function* in its branding line.

17.4.5 Are You Promising Too Much?

Can your position be sustained over the long run? In the first decade of the 21st century, NBC could truthfully tout itself as "the network of the Olympics." However, very few stations have an investment that will run that long. Your audience will soon determine if you're promising them the moon and delivering mud balls. Make sure your positioning line will outlive the morning paper.

17.4.6 Can Your Competition Steal Your Thunder?

Make sure that your competitors can't undermine your statement. In a classic case, at the turn of the last century, a beer company in New York City came up with the statement "We sterilize our bottles!" Of course, all the other brewers also sterilized their bottles, but being the first to say so effectively shut out competition until one competitor came up with "super-sterilized containers." If you are hawking the benefits of your helicopter, be aware that your competition can come up with a newer, faster, see-in-the-dark, and track-down-running-criminals machine. Be prepared.

17.4.7 Can You Introduce It Gradually?

A well-known axiom of human behavior notes that people hate changes, so if you are re-branding your station, make the changes gradually. If possible, make the changes consistent with prior associations, thereby positioning them as improvements. An example would be a new news set that will make it easier for the audience to see the weather or story preparation.

17.4.8 Are You Alienating Your Loyalists?

Another axiom of human behavior states it is easier to retain your current brand loyalists than it is to convince someone to change to your brand. Therefore, when making and implementing your branding statement, be sure you appreciate those loyalists. Even if their demographic isn't as valuable to the sales department, they have influence over demographics that are.

17.4.9 Will It Withstand the Test of Time?

The world's greatest brands have maintained the same position for decades. Just ask Coke, Betty Crocker, or Heinz. Can your positioning statement stand up that long? There is another oft-quoted axiom that by the time you—in the station—have gotten tired of a spot, it is just beginning to make a dent in the hearts and minds of the audience. How many times did you hear a Coke jingle before you realized you were thirsty and needed a Coke?

17.4.10 Does It Work in Copy?

This last item is one that will set the teeth of many creative people on edge. Make sure your positioning line can be easily and effectively translated into promotional spots and advertising copy. If you have decided to be "the bright and happy station," how will that line fit into a spot about hurricane death and destruction?

Work it out in copy, and if you determine that in some cases it would not be appropriate, make sure the copy restrictions are written down and understood by all those responsible for copy.

Likewise, see how the line works graphically. It may be great in a large-sized logo, but how does it look as a lower third? What happens to it in print as a "bug" in a co-op ad? What does it look like as a microphone flag with flags of your competition all around it?

17.5   SETTING OBJECTIVES AND STRATEGIES

The simple answer to starting work on the positioning line is this: Research. To know how to speak to your audience, you must know them inside and out.

A typical research project to accomplish something of this magnitude will include several focus groups and a large-universe either telephone or intercept interview process. There are a number of resources on how this is done, so we won't go into detail here.

Your research project came back, and over several days of exhaustive discussions in a room off-site you determined these highlights:

The audience is aware of your station, but only barely.

Your other network competition occupies their top of mind, and your station comes in when the interviewer probes.

The good news for you is that you're ahead of the WB and PAX affiliates.

Your audience tends to think in terms of the programs they see on your air. You are not FOX 33 to a large number of them. You are "football station" or "The Simpsons station" or "the station with the police chases." And to some, you're still known as "W-Good."

The public feels the news is already saturated with news.

They especially hate "body bag" news, but the numbers say they watch it.

The station has a deserved reputation for technical gaffes. It once sat on a slide for 15 minutes while a projector was being fixed during a local prime time movie.

You, the management (including the department heads), and your consultants huddle some more and come up with a list of branding lines. You do some more research to test them and come out with: "FOX 33, Sending Our Best"

The research shows that the public likes this line because

- It is simple and easily understood.
- Your station identity (FOX 33) is maintained.
- It doesn't boast.
- It doesn't over-deliver.
- It will be true for a long time no matter your position in the market.
- Your competition can't undermine it.
- It can be easily used in copy and graphics.
- It shows a certain amount of humility (or emotion).
- It has a bright promise for the future (be it in programming, news, or technical improvements).

17.6   DESIRED EFFECTS

To start the process of brand acceptance, your first step is to build brand awareness. This is the phase of the process that will consume much (but not all) of your resources.

17.6.1   On-Air Graphics

Set out to design the brand for both on- and off-air use. Your designer should preferably know television and print or have access to someone who does. The graphic's animation must meet the technical requirements of your equipment. Your animation house (or in-house computer graphics expert) will ask you to list all the applications. These will include the following:

- On-air identification (ID) animation as a stand-alone piece
- Promo open and close animation; interstitial (bump) animation
- Specialized applications you and your client users (i.e., news and sales) have developed
- Animated bugs for IDs

Spending the money now for top-quality, well-planned animation will save you and your station thousands of dollars and man hours down the road. Resist, if you can, the sales manager's brother-in-law who has a hot new graphics card in his computer and "can do as well as the big houses at a fraction of the cost." Animation has come a long way, but not quite that long.

17.6.2   Off-Air Graphics

Because you are starting a news operation, you are typically going to want to brand your news equipment up to and including your vehicles (unless you are in a market in which using a logo makes your vehicles targets). Your designer should be able to mock up how the logo will look on a variety of equipment. How does it looks in print, both newspaper and outdoor? Does it hold up when it is reduced to 8 points?

17.6.3   Music

A brand can be easily identified and retained by the audience if they hear it as well as see it. A music house experienced in working with television stations will work with you to write lyrics that will help the brand develop. They will also know what lengths of music are typically used on air. Any time you run the animated ID, you should also hear the music. You can also use seasonal variations of the music. For example, just adding the proverbial jingle bells will turn it into a holiday cut.

17.6.4   Printed Matter

Does the letterhead, business card, and other printed inventory of your station have your branding? Make sure that even the little printed message on your postage meter reflects your brand position.

17.7   KICK IT OFF–AND LISTEN

"X-Day" is the first day on which you start your branding roll-out. If your market research shows that the audience responds to personal messages, ask the general manager to tape a spot explaining "WFXX's new commitment to the audience" as embodied in your branding. Have her invite the audience to give her feedback by mail, fax, recorded phone message, or e-mail. Answer these communications with a brief, hand-signed message. This simple but key process will keep your loyalists from abandoning the station simply because they will feel that you are at least listening to their concerns. This same message can be put into a one-time newspaper ad.

The logo, animation, and music should be supported with your promo copy. In the case of WFXX, all promo spots end with "FOX 33, Sending Our Best." So a promo for the mythical syndicated program *Computer Nerds Get a Clue* will end with "Catch the fun tonight at 7 on FOX 33, Sending Our Best."

Once WFXX has kicked off this process of establishing the brand, keep the pressure up (Remember how many times you saw Heinz 57 before it made an impact). The WFXX branding process is no exception. Slowly, day by day, it will creep into the burgeoning awareness curve of your viewers. Your younger viewers will likely become aware of it first.

17.8   WHAT YOU MUST DO TO ESTABLISH THE BRAND

The "WFXX, Sending Our Best" line must be on everything the station does. Every vehicle should have the brand built into the logo; every satellite dish, microwave antenna, and camera should have it. Every promo, every public service announcement (PSA), every local program ending, every radio spot, every print ad, every outdoor poster, every banner, every hand-out, every brochure, every business card, every sales presentation, every everything.

This branding process is not only external; it must be carried forward to the staff. Every bulletin board should have "WFXX, Sending Our Best" somewhere on it. Every tape box, internal run-down sheet, message pad, and even screen saver on every office and newsroom computer needs to carry this message. The hold "music" on the internal phone system should have the "Sending Our Best" music jingle on it. Every eyeball and every eardrum should have this message wash over it at sometime during the day, whenever people make contact with the brand.

The on-air product, too, must meet the needs of your target audience. Your extensive research has delineated their wants, needs, and desires. Focus groups, shopping center intercept interviews, and telephone interviews should provide a vivid picture of the audience. The challenge is to position the brand in such a way as to convince the audience that the station will at least assist them in fulfilling their wants, needs, and desires.

The branding of the on-air product goes beyond promos, IDs, PSAs, and radio spots. It extends into the selection of news stories that will be promoted and teased throughout the day. Although it is not necessary to have the newscasters per se say "Sending Our Best," the branding may be accomplished in both tangible and intangible ways. A promo tag line such as "If you have children, you won't want to miss this story" immediately plants in the mind of the potential viewer (who may or may not have kids) the desire to see the story. More importantly, it establishes the brand in the audience's mind as someone who cares about children and the needs of their parents.

Market research shows that the viewers are available and willing to watch the 10:00 p.m. news. Focus group feedback tells the station the audience doesn't want a newscast just like all the others. The news director agrees to structure the news somewhat unconventionally, allowing the brand manager to call it "different."

The television on-air will start 5 weeks from premiere date with a 5-day tease using 10-second spots exclusively: "Something DIFFERENT is coming. FOX 33, Sending Our Best." The spot campaign will expand during the next 4 weeks as the anchors are introduced in the news room talking about how they have listened to what the market has said and that they will be part of the "difference." The spots always end with "FOX 33, Sending Our Best."

For WFXX's 10:00 p.m. news, radio will be used to continue to build brand awareness: "There's a different kind of newscast in town, and it's on a different station. FOX 33, Sending Our Best."

Outdoor designs will highlight the "different" branding aspect as well as "Sending Our Best."

The brand manager puts the anchors on the road, speaking to civic clubs about how they love the market and how exciting it is to be part of something different. The brand manager always makes sure there are plenty of hand-outs available with anchor pictures and branding statement.

The weatherman sets up a schedule of speaking to school science classes about meteorology and leaves behind handouts with anchor pictures and the brand statement.

This campaign, both on and off air, continues to premiere date with radio and print peaking on that date.

The headlines on the PAX station have the PAX logo on screen, but your station's talent ID as "Sarah Slade, WFXX Metro News @ 11." The marketing of your product on their air is something that must be continually researched and monitored.

Once WFXX has kicked this branding off, keep the pressure up. Remember how many times Heinz 57 varieties was seen or heard before it made an impact. Your branding process is no exception. Slowly, day by day, it will creep into the burgeoning awareness curve of your viewers. Younger viewers will likely become aware of it first.

From here, the savvy brand manager can chart his or her own course using the principles in this book, checking themselves against the practices as they build toward the future.

18 | Dealing with the Digital World

As society makes the transition from one form of entertainment delivery to a newer one, our standard thinking is constantly challenged. Our business models are destroyed. And yesterday suddenly becomes one of those good old days. Note how the motion picture studios battled against first the encroachment of television, then the ubiquitous VCR, and now the even more ubiquitous DVD player.

In June 1989, a speaker at the Detroit PROMAX Convention (then known as the Broadcast Promotion Marketing Executives, or BPME) predicted that this newly emerging technology of digital delivery would revolutionize the industry. He told the skeptical attendees that a full-length motion picture could be digitally delivered to their home in a matter of minutes and watched a finite number of times and then would disappear. He also told them about something called the Digital Versatile Disc, which could hold many hours of high-quality video and numerous stunning soundtracks. The presenter's name is lost to history, but his predictions are not. Just ask Time Warner, Net Flicks, and George Lucas.

At the time, home video players cost in the neighborhood of $500 to $1,000. The motion picture industry was reluctantly releasing product on the format. Mom & Pop video rental stores were appearing in every strip mall. Viewers were discovering the joys and challenges of time shifting and VCRs with blinking 12:00 a.m. clocks.

Not many knew it at the time, but the old way of business was being reconsidered.

In the early days, these new-fangled PCs had as much as 10 MB of disk space and a whopping 128 kb of memory. Some even had VGA (video graphics array) color cards and could, at various odd times, run Windows 1.1. If equipped with a bulky modem, they could actually use the phone lines to reach bulletin boards and exchange messages. Or something.

That was then.

This is now.

Now, as marketing executives, we must find ways not only to deal with things digital but also to innovate with them. Once this book is published, the ideas here are static, but the world will go on. Use, if you will, some of these suggestions to be a jumping-off point for your thinking. You and your team, after all, are on the bleeding edge of innovation. Make the most of it.

18.1   MULTICASTING—THE DIGITAL SLIPSTREAM

With your station's digital slipstream of additional standard broadcast signals, you have the opportunity to narrowcast to specific audiences. The sales department has already come up with the Used Car Channel, the Apartment Finder Channel, the All Infomercial Channel, the Watching Paint Dry Channel, and other projects limited only by your equipment.

But what can you do to market yourself along this digital slipstream? And who's watching? We'll leave the second question to be wrestled with by the researchers, but the first question is a key to your marketing plans.

Many stations feed their weather radar over their slipstream. Does yours? Some stations have repeats of the last newscast playing over and over until the next news time period. Do you?

Ask yourself what product is available to be multicast within the emerging economics of the expanding number of available channels? What product will work within the station's marketing objectives to drive audiences to the main channel? What messages can go on the multicast channels to effectively gather audiences?

Technology has given you another few canvases to paint. Can you fill them with great images?

18.2   THE UBIQUITOUS DVD

Until the next one comes along, it's safe to say that no product has made such a tremendous impact on modern entertainment as has the DVD. Once Hollywood got over its trepidations, it became the entertainment format of choice after the films' first run. (And, for some less-than-sterling films, it became the "video" in the direct-to-video consolation prize.) The virtual acres of space on the disc invite spectacular presentations. The cost of manufacturing the discs has plummeted, inviting more use of the format. Players' prices have nose-dived along with the cost of the disks.

How can you, as a television station, use it? Why would you want to?

Taking the second question first: you must always look for another way into the hearts and minds of your viewers to keep them loyal to your station. The DVD allows you to do so.

There are a number of ways to use it, but the one that will pay off most handsomely in terms of ratings and sales is to cater to newcomers. For decades, newcomers were greeted by the Welcome Wagon. When that business model succumbed to the changing economy, other ways were explored, most involving direct mail.

A newcomers' DVD will permit you to get your product(s) into the homes of people who may not have made their choices for local news and entertainment. It will permit you to showcase your on-air talent in a genial and helpful way as they explain your market's appealing facets and give tips to the newbies.

Your sales department could have a field day with the sales possibilities. First, they would do well to tie in to your market's largest realtor. Real estate agencies have a very active list of who is moving into the area. Make sure your DVD is included in the packages they send to out of town requests. Then work your way through the list of commercial establishments who want to be exposed to newcomers. But always–keep your on-air product tied in. The sales potential from this one project could be tremendous.

18.3   ONLINE

It's hard to believe that in the 1990s, many stations were disinclined to have a presence on this new thing called the Internet. Webheads were clamoring to deaf ears about all the neat things that could go on a station's Web page. Now, a station without a Web presence is literally living in the last century. It would be redundant to list what you can do on the Web in these pages, because the technology to do things is improving relentlessly. Your station's computer guru will be happy to point you to some of the most innovative sites available. And give you her own ideas for improving them.

Legal Issues Surrounding Branding: Branding and the Law

Steven J. Dick, Ph.D

A brand is the cutting edge of the corporate identity. It may be the only part of a marketing effort that breaks through to customer, and it is absolutely necessary that it breaks through cleanly. Although the rest of this book discusses how to *create* a brand, this chapter looks at how to *protect* it as a corporate asset. After all the effort to create a brand, it would be a shame to lose your work because of the actions of someone else. In many cases, legal help will be necessary to interpret your specific situation. However, this chapter should give you the general idea.

In the days of the old American West, branding quite literally meant to burn a logo into your product (cattle). It separated your product from the herd. Your brand did not need to be artistic or even original. It only had to be unique to your cattle. Today, trademark law has the same goal. The goal is to make it clear to all which product comes from which supplier. A proper appreciation for trademark law helps to protect your branding effort and those of your competitors.

19.1 INTELLECTUAL PROPERTY

Television lives on intellectual property—intangible products produced enterprises of the mind. Although we may understand the essentials of copyright, other forms of intellectual property are more difficult. There are four classes of intellectual property. A full discussion is a book in itself. Although the rest of this chapter will look at trademark, there are three other types of protections that *may* impact branding.

19.2   INTELLECTUAL PROPERTY PROTECTION

Copyright protects an expression, not just an idea. Original artwork or copy can be protected by copyright. Copyright protection is enforced when the work rises to the level of a unique expression of an idea, concept, or work of art. Most brands, slogans, and trademarks are usually too small to rise to the level of copyright protection. It is difficult to argue that "tri-state news leader" is not just an idea.

Normally, we think of patents protecting inventions created in the back room of a laboratory. However, a design patent is possible on the specific product. Design patents are normally assigned to items such as silverware or the "look" of a tangible product. A station promotion simply would not qualify for this level of protection.

Trade secrets include information that is not generally known or shared. All proprietary data, processes, and some databases (such as contact lists) may be protected by trade secrets. The main purpose of trade secrets is to keep an employee from leaving your company and taking essential elements of the business with them. An overall brand strategy may be considered a trade secret but not the logos or slogans.

19.3   INTENT OF LAW

The protection of intellectual property is split between creative and business considerations. Copyright and patent protections are designed to encourage creative activity. These policies give the creator powerful control over products. The focus of the law is on the product. The controlling legal question is "Who created the product and when?" Generally, the first person to create a product gets the exclusive right to profit from it.

Trademark and trade secrets regulate the business relationship. Instead of protecting unique ideas, the goal is to protect businesses from each other. The controlling legal question becomes "Are profits lost or customers deceived?" If the answer is "no," almost everything else should become a non-issue.

Creativity is not protected as much as business investment in these "business protection" statutes. The underlying assumption is that competition works best when customers are clear as to the source of products. Two people can not patent the same process; however, two people can use the same brand image as long as they do not interfere with one another.

Because the value of trademarks is driven more by market forces than inherent value, protection is more of an art than an assurance. The person wishing to protect a mark should consider several factors, including functions, strength, and registration of the mark. Together these factors can determine the effectiveness of your protection.

19.4   USE OF A TRADEMARK

The trademark is used to distinguish your station in the market, indicate source, and represent goodwill. A violation will mislead the public and interfere with any of these functions. How do the stations in *your* market distinguish themselves from one another? Although you are not locked in to this history, it helps to show *your* goodwill or *others'* attempts to deceive. In some markets, the stations may present themselves in distinctly different ways from each other. In others, the stations may have a very similar pattern of promotion. Historically, the courts assume people will see and understand the real differences when it is part of the tradition in that market.

Pay particular attention to branding protections during periods of network switches in the market. Branding can become a problem and is more important at these times. Consumers do not understand the difference between network and syndicated programming. In addition, some stations may hold ill-will over the changes and thus attempt to mock, block, or confuse the audience moving to a competitor.

Goodwill is the real point of branding. If another station is using your goodwill to sell their product, that may be a violation of your trademark. This does not necessarily stop a person from making fun of you or your product, but it does stop them from diverting your work into their product.

19.5   "WHAT" MARK?

There are three related categories included under the broad concept of trademark. Strictly speaking, "trademarks" are names for tangible products only. For example, Ampex has a trademark on its brand of video tape. Because television stations provide an intangible service, their brands are protected as a "service mark." In the United States, there is virtually no difference in the protection provided. Internationally, you may see a difference.

A corporate name, such as WXXX, Inc., can be protected as a "trade name." The essential difference is that the trademarks (service marks) describe your product—not all broadcasting but Cosmos Broadcasting. Trade names are more inclusive. Thus, it is easier to protect Cosmos Television than Cosmos, Inc. This is especially true when the trade name has literal meaning. NBC is easier to protect than National Broadcasting Company.

A corporation my have all three. Ampex, Inc. may provide Ampex video tape and Ampex Duplication Services. The company is protected by trade name. The tape is protected by trademark and the service by service mark. Except for a lesser protection given to trade names, the concepts are pretty similar. In this chapter, trademark is used as a generic.

19.6   STRONG VERSUS WEAK MARKS

As discussed above, some names are easier to defend than are others. The relative ability of a brand to be associated only with a corporation is called the strength of the brand. For example, Kodak is a strong trademark because it has no meaning outside of the product. Center City Television, on the other hand, is simply descriptive. Customers may know the *company* but the *mark* is harder to defend. The new company Center City Radio may successfully argue that it does not infringe on the earlier trademark.

You may think of trademarks as a continuum from strongest to weakest:

◆ *Fanciful names* are those words devoid of meaning outside the company, such as Kodak or Polaroid.

◆ *Arbitrary names* have meaning but not meaning associated with the product, such as Touchstone or Apple.

◆ *Suggestive names* have meaning somewhat associated with the product, such as the Storm Team or Weather Friends.

◆ *Descriptive names* simply state what the product is in simple terms, such as Mississippi Broadcasting or the *Six O'clock News*.

◆ *Generic words,* channel 6 or television, can not be trademarked by themselves.

A weak trademark can still be defended. It is just harder. The company must show that they have invested in the name and that the name has acquired secondary meaning in the public. If you are using Storm Team, for example, it is a fairly weak trademark. You must show that your audience understands that the Storm Team is on channel 6 and the Weather Friends are on another channel. Weak trademarks will also face greater challenges if the company wishes to extend the brand to a national or international market. For example, "Southwest Broadcasting" may have problems from "Southwest Airlines." The

Federal Register of Trademarks may reject a trademark outright that is too weak.

Television stations are in a unique position. The very descriptive name WXXX-TV 12 can still be fanciful. Normally the call letters are unique in the public's mind. A problem arises when a new station takes on call letters similar to a station already in the market. KLBP may be forced to defend its name when KBPL enters the market. The Federal Communications Commission (FCC) stopped negotiating these disputes in the 1980s. Now, it is simply a trademark matter. Stations should be vigilant as new competitors enter the market.

19.7 SLOGANS

Unique names and slogans receive the same trademark protection as logos and should be defended just as carefully. Disputes may often arise over slogans and jingles. Slogans are too short for effective copyright protection. Even if you could copyright "Eyewitness News," a competitor would have equal reason to copyright "Your Witness News." Trademark protection steps in to protect slogans the same as logos.

With slogans, you must go back to why we have trademarks in the first place. Trademark law does not give ownership rights, just exclusive-use rights. There is no problem with 100 Eyewitness News stations in this country, but there *is* a problem with two in one market. Even if you buy your promotion package from a national distributor, you may have a problem if it tends to confuse the audience.

19.8 DILUTION

A strong brand gives the company that owns it not only an economic advantage but also a legal advantage. The more clearly the audience perceives an association between a trademark and a *specific* program, the stronger the protection. But as stations start multi-channel broadcasting, they may be tempted to extend their traditional brands into the new services. Thus, brands such as ESPN get extended into ESPN2, ESPN College, or ESPN Oldies. Stations may also dilute their own brand by changing slogans or logo colors. Each time these trademarks are changed, the clock on their use practically restarts. Because older trademarks are stronger than newer ones, the station dilutes it own protection as it dilutes its brands.

In 1996, the Federal Trademark Act was amended to provide federal protection against trademark dilution. As stated above, confusion has always been the standard but this Act provides for owners of famous trademarks to keep people from using their mark in a way that simply dilutes the brand's identity. The issue here is not so much consumer confusion but a loss of distinction. The basic argument is that these lawsuits protect their corporate image. Before this law, Campbell Soup and Campbell broadcast could both exist. No one was confused. Under the law, a new company named Campbell Broadcasting may be challenged because it dilutes the power of the name Campbell. Because the law is so new, it has not been properly tested. We have yet to see the definition of "famous" trademarks and how powerfully the courts interpret the law.

A disturbing new trend in recent years is a group of aggressive lawsuits claiming *brand dilution*. Dairy Queen used the technique to discourage a producer from using their corporate name as a movie title (American Dairy Queen Corp. v. New Line Productions, Inc.). Although there was no association between the movie and the ice cream company, Dairy Queen argued that the movie would degrade their corporate image. In even more aggressive cases, the technique has been used as a counter-attack technique. Perhaps the most visible brand dilution case was launched by the Fox News cable channel. Fox claimed that the comic and writer Al Franken (Fox News Network, LLC v. Penguin Group [USA], Inc.) violated its trademark when he used the phrase "fair and balanced" in a book title. The end result was both embarrassing for the cable channel and expensive for the comic.

19.9   SOURCES OF DISPUTE

Although it is more difficult to establish (especially in the fast changing media world), mediated products can be addressed under a larger "trade dress" concept. Traditional trade dress protects the overall look of a McDonald's restaurant versus that of a Hardees. For example, John Deere defended the use of its unique shade of green as part of its trademark (Deere & Co. v. MTD Products, Inc). Special jingles and characters can have the same effect if they are central to the station's operation or programming. Even if the station does not own the copyright on a jingle, it may have trademark protection. One can easily imagine several songs that brings a specific program to mind.

Disputes over specialty characters are normally associated with radio. For example, a station may build a promotional effort around the made-up character "Jimmy the Frog," and a competitive station may be kept from creating a deceptively similar character. These characters result in a confusing mix of trademark and copyright disputes. David Letterman's switch from NBC to CBS raised disputes concerning some of his specialty characters. Barney, the children's program, invited an onslaught of purple dinosaur costumes for children's parties.

Trademark problems may grow in an era of consolidation and multi-channel broadcasting. Broadcast outlets and audiences will face a dizzying array of program sources. The temptation may be for a station to co-brand a programming. For example, if an NBC affiliate co-owns a WB station, the promotions department may be tempted to combine promos. This may make perfect sense to the promotions department and the audience. However, the trademark owners (NBC and WB) may not be so understanding.

19.10   REGISTRATION

The bad news is that trademark registration can be a pain. It is expensive, complicated, and time consuming. In the end, you may not get the trademark you wanted. The good news is that full registration is usually not needed for a local television station. Although it offers additional protections and puts possible offenders on notice, it is not needed to defend your rights. As the broadcast market changes, companies should anticipate the day that they will need national registration—just in case.

The first level of protection comes from simply using your trademark in commerce. A trademark that is used has the upper hand on a trademark that is planned—no matter which was written first. Using your mark gives you common law protection in the geographic area of your station. This means that neither a local nor national company can come into your market to take your mark.

You can register your trademark with your state (or states). The registration may not do you much good, but it does not cost much either. Usually, the state will only check if the identical mark is already registered and add your mark to the database. You may gain certain procedural advantages because it also looks like you're doing the right thing. State registration may be enough to scare off some competitors or impress a judge. In a tough case, however, it does not mean much.

You can get a strong national protection from federal registration with the U.S. Patents and Trademarks Office. Registration can put others on notice that the mark belongs to you. It increases penalties and gives some international protection and Internet protection. You may also register an "intent to use" for a trademark up to 3 years in advance.

Federal registration can also be expensive. The process can easily take more than a year and cost thousands. You must perform your own search for anyone else using your mark. An overlooked contender to your mark can send you back to the beginning at any time. Professional help is a necessity. Despite the risks, national registration can mean a big payoff if you plan to commit to your mark on a national scale.

International protection is for seasoned veterans and well beyond the space allowed here. It could take a minimum of 3 years. Not all countries recognize international protection and fewer enforce it. It is a step that should not be made lightly or without assistance.

19.11   INTERNET

Local television stations are local by nature and technology. The main reason to consider expanded trademark protection is the Internet. This argument has merit but may be simplistic. Putting your product out on the Internet pushes your product from a regional to international market. If you are going to build a campaign, you want to protect your investment. You may also open yourself up as a defendant by going beyond your normal geographic market.

However, thousands of stations face the same dilemma. Some names will be unavailable—Amazon and ESPN Sportzone, for example. Other names may need to be more specific—*Lansing's* Eyewitness News. Litigation is likely but so is compromise. Major questions may start when the American ABC faces direct competition from the Australian ABC.

Competition will depend on how you define your market. Are you really going to market to the whole world or just your region (and expatriates)? Many stations run a telephone information service (e.g., time and temperature). It has a potential world-wide audience but not a practical world-wide audience. The Internet can deliver that audience easier, but is that your audience? It comes back to market confusion. Are people going to confuse your Louisiana service with the one from Canada?

A bigger problem is the products you buy. Can you tolerate your syndicated promo package used by 100 other people on the Internet? Can they tolerate you? Do you have the right in your syndication contract to use it online? Converting product to the Internet means converting it to another media. Do you have the right for non-television distribution? The Internet is an intellectual property quagmire because products sold to you were intended for local distribution. Most syndication contracts were written before the Internet's explosion of popularity.

Universal resource locators (URLs) have become the center of most disputes on the Internet. These names, most commonly used as Web page and e-mail addresses, are generally allocated on a first-come basis. This has caused WXXX broadcasting to fight with the WXXX corporation for the URL WXXX.com. Beyond normal disputes, cyber-squatters attempt to claim URLs only to resell them to a corporation. Other entrepreneurs claim similar URLs and misspellings of popular URLs. For example, Viacom.com may need to fight the owner of Vacomm.com (without the "i"). To the extent the second URL appears to be the first, a trademark battle may develop.

Finally, protest sites have developed for many corporations. The URL might be WXXXsucks.com. To a certain extent, these sites have been discouraged by brand dilution lawsuits. However, attacking protest sites may have a backlash as the public perceives a rich corporation battling with a poor protester. Further, trademark law is poorly designed to combat free speech (see next section).

19.12   FAIR COMMENT

When Jim Henson decided to add a new character to his beloved Muppets, he pleased everyone but Hormel. The new character, a pig called Spa'am, was not exactly complimentary to Spam, the trademarked product by Hormel. Hormel felt compelled to defend its mark. However, the court ruled in favor of the Muppets because the Muppets use was parody and could not be taken seriously.

As much as it displeases us, we have invited people to watch our product. Therefore, they have the right to comment on its quality. Fair comment is allowed. Many corporations have used trademark law (some successfully) to squash comment. In fairness, the question should be, "Are people deceived by the use of your trademark?" No one could really believe the Muppets were selling ham or Spam. The result is fair comment on the product.

19.13   PROTECTION

Some companies seem overly aggressive in defending their trademarks. Although corporate culture may cause them to be naturally more aggressive in business deals, the problem comes more from logic than attitude. A company that fails to defend its trademarks can lose them entirely. At best, the company loses some protection. At worst, the trademark name can be completely lost or become the generic name for the product.

Trademark protection can be difficult especially if you aggressively defend everything. A wimpy approach is not necessary, but it can be easy to assume a violation that is too minor to defend. Most of us, after all, are not in the trademark business. Trademarks are tools that are used and reused. Valuable trademarks must be defended. In the fast-paced changes of our industry, it may be best to give up on others.

Despite the trouble, a trademark protection plan is valuable. Such a plan would have six stages:

1. Know your market
2. Know your station
3. Record keeping
4. Registration
5. Audience awareness
6. Action/cooperation

19.13.1   Know Your Market

If you are going to defend your marks, you must not do it by stepping on the rights of others. A good trademark policy starts by understanding your market. How do the customers differentiate products? How diverse are the products? What marks are being used? Remember, television markets differ. The audience in one market may see things differently from your last station.

19.13.2   Know Your Station

Your station is full of creative people, and they create valuable products full time. Actively evaluate ongoing creations for exploitation. Is it just another weathercast or a valuable opportunity? Are your people stealing ideas from competitors? Pay particular attention to stringers, contractors, and part-timers. Have they taken something that does not belong to them? Do you own their creations? Identify your best products for exploitation and start the process. Make your policy clear and known to avoid misunderstanding. Use internal memos and press releases to advertise your policy when needed.

19.13.3   Record Keeping

First use in commerce is valuable to trademark. First creation is valuable in copyright. Accurate records bolster any claim. When was it first created? How was it developed and by whom? What changes were made and when? How much money was spent? These records are valuable ammunition for later litigation.

19.13.4   Trademark Registration

When warranted, register your trademark early and often. Register it for all potential uses (service mark, trademark, trade name) and in all potential markets. If your signal crosses state lines, so does your trademark. If you need national or international registration, start the process.

19.13.5   Audience Awareness

A trademark's value hinges on audience understanding. Can you show you have achieved that valuable "secondary meaning" or brand identification? Where, when, and how strong is it? This information helps not only your branding effort but your ability to defend the trademark.

19.13.6   Action

Where appropriate, defend your trademark vigorously. We want people to understand and like the mark but we want it correct. Trademarks are strongest when you are absolutely fanatical about expressing it exactly the same way every time: no poor uncontrolled reproductions of the logo, no cute variations on the slogan. Never let anyone use it unless it is clear that the work belongs to you. If you do not seem to care about your trademark, neither will the courts.

Cooperation is tricky in light of anti-trust laws. However, the cheapest trade—mark protection is out of court. Your competitors are doing just the same as you-trying to identify and differentiate their product. It is more productive, when possible, to take each station's promotion in a different direction and *not* constantly step on each other's brands.

19.14   CONCLUSION

This chapter was intended to give you an overview of trademark policy and some strategies for protection. You should take it for what it is—a warning and a starting point. Your station's lawyers are needed to tailor your own brand strategy.

Your brands can be valuable, and they are worth protecting. You need to build your brand strategy on solid ground and protect it as you would any other investment. A good understanding of the trademark law can be just as valuable as a good understanding of branding.

20 The Future: Limitless Choice and
CHAPTER the Future of TV Branding

Although media technology will continue to evolve at an ever-increasing pace, the fundamental tenets of human nature will not. The prospect of limitless choice brought on by the marvels of technology and deregulation is both enticing and intimidating. The good news is that there will be enormous variety, the bad news is that audiences will soon realize that sometimes you can have too much of a good thing. Consumers have neither the time nor the patience to deal with today's proliferation of products, services, and media options. The novelty of channel surfing and random sampling of program content will soon surrender to some means of creating order out of chaos. Over time, audiences will develop a smaller and more manageable program inventory or "brand repertoire" of media brands that possess a strong, favorable, and unique *reputation*.

Regardless of the source of the program content—broadcast television, cable, microwave, satellite, on-line, telephony, or some yet to be invented electronic delivery system—audiences will continue to seek program content that satisfies their needs and desires. In addition to appreciating functional benefits, such as information and guidance, audiences will also seek media brands that exude intangible or emotional payoffs. Also, advertisers and media buyers will be integrated more into the total brand equity of a media product. Business values, such as trust, integrity, honesty, and reliability, will be fused with the more conventional "audience delivery" factors.

The industry's current preoccupation with distribution technology will eventually take a back seat to the bigger issue of audience satisfaction based on content rather than hardware. Ongoing *media convergence* promises a future in which all program content will be seen on one screen by using one simple tuning device. The hardware of antennas, cable boxes, personal computers, satellite dishes, and telephones will become obsolete, giving way to all-purpose "appliances" that will access with a push of a button any content we want.

In some respects the cliché of the more things change, the more they remain the same is ironically true for the brave new world of electronic media. People don't watch technology, they watch television.

The catalyst for all our discussions about branding television has been the notion of competition, and in the coming years, introducing new media brands will be tougher in an already crowded marketplace. Similarly, maintaining brand equity for established brands will be tougher in a business arena filled with zealous challengers. To survive and prosper in this highly competitive environment, the art and science of television brand management will become ever more important.

We have presented some ideas and suggestions in this book, knowing that the human mind, with its limitless imagination, will perhaps find newer, more innovative ways of reaching any potential audience with the branding message. We have provided a platform. Dive in and have a ball!

The future is yours for the branding!

A | Recommended Reading

Aaker, D.A. (1991). *Managing Brand Equity: Capitalizing on the Value of a Brand Name.* New York: The Free Press.

Aaker, D.A. (2001). *Developing Business Strategies,* 6th ed. New York: John Wiley Publishing.

Bayan, R. (1987). *Words That Sell.* Chicago: Contemporary Books.

De Chernatony, L., McDonald, M. (2003). *Creating Powerful Brands.* Oxford, UK: Butterworth Heinemann.

Dickey, L. (1994). *The Franchise: Building Radio Brands.* Washington, DC: National Association of Broadcasters (NAB).

Eastman, S.E., Ferguson, D.A., Klein, R.A. (2002). *Promotion and Marketing for Broadcasting, Cable and the Web.* Boston, MA: Focal Press.

Hiebing, R.G., Cooper, S.W. (1994). *The Successful Marketing Plan: A Disciplined and Comprehensive Approach.* Lincolnwood, IL: NTC Business Books.

Kapferer, J.N. (1992). *Strategic Brand Management: New Approaches to Creating and Evaluating Brand Equity.* New York: The Free Press.

Keller, K.L. (2003). *Strategic Brand Management: Building, Measuring and Managing Brand Equity.* Upper Saddle River, NJ: Prentice Hall.

Ries, A., Trout, J. (1980). *Positioning: The Battle for Your Mind.* New York: McGraw-Hill.

Von Oech, R. (1986). *A Kick in the Seat of the Pants.* New York: Harper & Row.

Von Oech, R. (1998). *A Whack on the Side of the Head : How You Can Be More Creative.* New York: Warner Books

Webster, J.G., Phalen, P., Lichty, L.W. (2000). *Ratings Analysis: The Theory and Practice of Audience Research.* Hillsdale, NJ: Lawrence Erlbaum Associates.

Werz, E., Germain, S.(1998) *Phrases That Sell: The Ultimate Phrase Finder to Help You Promote Your Products, Services, and Ideas.* Chicago: Contemporary Books.

Yoffie, D.B., Kwak, M. (2001). *Judo Strategy: Turning Your Competitor's Strength to Your Advantage.* Boston, MA: Harvard Business School Press.

Zyman, S. (1999). *The End of Marketing as We Know It.* New York: Harper Business.

Basic Training: How To Read A Rating Book

Alan Batten

One of the things a television brand manager has to deal with every day is the ratings. But many people may either never learned how or have forgotten how to read a rating book, so here's a refresher course.

The Nielsen Media Research company compiles diary ratings four times a year in most markets. (Larger markets have additional rating books in October and January, and four markets have an additional rating opportunity in March.) Nielsen is also responsible for overnight measurements in a growing number of markets.

Let's look at a typical rating book containing data from diaries. The first, and most obvious place to start is the designated market area, or DMA. Your station serves these people. But it serves some better than others. The counties in white are your metro counties. This is the key segment of the market. The metro is surrounded by what are called your local DMA counties. The fringe DMA counties may also view signals from other markets but, in Nielsen's opinion, they view your market the most. And the entire map gives you a general feeling for where you are in relation to other markets.

Now that you know where your station is, you want to find out about ratings and shares. You generally will be most concerned with your station's ratings and shares in a given period.

What is a rating? According to Nielsen it is "the percentage of a population viewing a TV program during an average time slice." That so-called time slice is anywhere between 15 minutes and half an hour, depending on the time of day.

The other important number is share. According to Nielsen, a share of audience is the percentage of television usage attributable to a program.

You also need to pay attention to the homes using television (HUT) column and the people using television (PUT) column. They tell you how big your universe is.

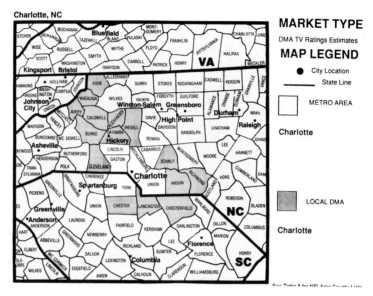

FIGURE

B-1

A typical DMA map. Courtesy Nielsen Media Research.

Statistically minded brand managers can derive the share by dividing the rating by the HUT. Or get the rating by multiplying the share times the HUT. Or get the HUT by dividing the rating by the share. For your purposes, however, the most stable number of the three is the share of audience to provide a rough comparison of program popularity. But there are a lot more numbers on this page than rating, share, and HUTs.

What good are they? Your station sells these rating points to advertisers. A given advertiser may know that women between the ages of 18 and 34 are most likely to buy its product. So your sales department sells the advertiser a program that has a high particular demographic. How your station does in the desirable demos (demographics) can make or break a sales goal. Because the marketing department can be called the station's chief advertiser, it's your goal to attract as many of these desirable demos as possible. So, know your demos! Are your programs strong in men? Women? Children? A few moments studying the demographic column should give you a picture of where your station is relative to others in your market.

How often and how well you reach these people with your message is called "reach and frequency." Reach and frequency data can't be determined from standard ratings book. But you should know what the terms *reach* and *frequency* mean. Reach is the number of different homes or people exposed at least once to your

CHARLOTTE, NC

MONDAY-FRIDAY 6:00PM - 9:00PM

WK1 2/05-2/11 WK2 2/12-2/18 WK3 2/19-2/25 WK4 2/26-3/04

METRO HH RTG	METRO HH SHR	STATION	PROGRAM	DMA HOUSEHOLD RATINGS WEEKS 1	2	3	4	MULTI-WEEK AVG RTG	SHR	SHARE TREND NOV	MAY	FEB
1 LT			R.S.E. THRESHOLDS 25+% (1 S.E.) 4 WK AVG 50+%	1 LT	1 LT	1 LT	1 LT	1 LT				
		6:00PM										
1	2	WAXN	REAL-HWY PATRL	1	1	1	1	1	2	2X	2	2
11	21	WBTV	WBTV NWS-600P	13	11	12	12	12	22	24X	25	26
2	4	WCCB	MARTIN	3	2	2	2	2	4	5	7	8
5	9	WCNC	6 NEWS AT 6PM	3	4	4	4	4	7	6X	5	4
2	4	WFVT	FRESH PRINCE	2	2	2	2	2	4	4	4	3
3	5	WJZY	GRACE-FIRE MF	3	4	3	3	3	6	6X	7	5
<<		WNSC	NEWSHOUR-LEHR	<<	<<	<<	<<	<<		1		1
21	38	WSOC	EYEWIT NWS 6	19	20	20	19	19	34	30X	30	32
<<		WTVI	VARIOUS	<<	<<	<<	<<	<<				
<<		WUNG	NEWSHOUR-LEHR	1	<<	1	<<	<<		1X		
55			HUT/PUT/TOTALS*	57	58	56	54	56		57	48	59
		6:30PM										
3	4	WAXN	JUDGE JUDY	3	3	3	3	3	4	6X	3	3
11	19	WBTV	CBS EVE NWS	11	11	11	11	11	19	20X	20	21
5	8	WCCB	SIMPSONS	4	4	4	4	4	7	5	7	8
5	9	WCNC	NBC NITELY NWS	4	5	4	4	4	7	7X	7	6
3	5	WFVT	HANGN-MR COOPR	3	3	3	2	3	5	4	5	5
4	7	WJZY	GRACE-FRE MF B	5	5	4	4	4	7	7X	8	7
<<		WNSC	NEWSHOUR-LEHR	<<	<<	<<	<<	<<				
17	29	WSOC	ABC WORLD NWS	15	16	16	15	15	26	24X	24	25
1	1	WTVI	VARIOUS	1	<<	1	<<	<<				
<<		WUNG	NEWSHOUR-LEHR	<<	<<	<<	<<	<<		X		
59			HUT/PUT/TOTALS*	60	61	58	57	59		58	49	60
		7:00PM										
4	6	WAXN	JUDGE JUDY B	3	3	4	4	3	6	8X	4	2
7	12	WBTV	ACCESS HOLLYWD	7	7	7	8	7	12	12X	13	14
6	9	WCCB	HOME IMPR MF B	6	6	5	5	5	9	9X	10	10
10	16	WCNC	JEOPARDY	9	9	9	8	9	14	15X	15	15
4	7	WFVT	LIVING SINGLE	4	3	3	4	3	6	6X	6	6
6	9	WJZY	SEINFELD	6	6	5	5	5	9	9X	8	8
<<		WNSC	NITE BSNSS RPT	<<	<<	<<	<<	<<				
12	20	WSOC	INSIDE EDITION	9	10	11	10	10	17	16X	17	17
1	1	WTVI	NEWSHOUR-LEHR	<<	<<	<<	<<	<<		X		
<<		WUNG	NITE BSNSS RPT	<<	<<	<<	<<	<<		X		
60			HUT/PUT/TOTALS*	62	63	60	60	61		60	50	62
		7:30PM										
4	6	WAXN	AVG ALL WKS	3	3	3	3	3	4	5	3	3
3	5		#REAL-HWY PATRL	3				3	4			
4	6		REAL-HWY PATRL		3	3	3	3	4			
7	11	WBTV	EXTRA	7	7	7	7	7	11	10X	12	13
7	11	WCCB	HOME IMPROV MF	7	7	6	6	6	10	10X	11	12
10	16	WCNC	WHEEL-FORTNE	9	11	11	9	10	16	17X	18	17
4	7	WFVT	AVG. ALL WKS	4	4	4	4	4	6	7	6	6
4	7		#FRESH PRINCE	4				4	6			
4	7		FRESH PRINCE		4	4	4	4	6			
6	9	WJZY	AVG. ALL WKS	6	6	4	6	5	8	8	8	7
6	9		#FRASIER	6		4		5	8			
6	9		FRASIER		6		6	6	9			
<<		WNSC	VARIOUS	<<	<<	<<	<<	<<				
13	21	WSOC	ENT TONIGHT 30	10	10	12	10	10	16	14X	15	14
<<		WTVI	NEWSHOUR-LEHR	<<	<<	<<	<<	<<		X		
<<		WUNG	NC NOW	<<	<<	<<	1	<<		1X	1	
63			HUT/PUT/TOTALS*	64	65	64	62	64		62	53	64

STATION	PROGRAM	DMA RATINGS PERSONS 2+	18+	12-24	12-34	18-34	18-49	21-49	25-54	35+	35-64	50+
	R.S.E. THRESHOLDS 25+% (1 S.E.) 4 WK AVG 50+%	1 LT	1 LT	4 1	2 LT	2 LT	1 LT	1 LT	1 LT	1 LT	1 LT	1 LT
6:00PM												
WAXN	REAL-HWY PATRL	1	1				1	1	1	1	1	2
WBTV	WBTV NWS-600P	7	9	1	4	4	6	6	7	11	8	14
WCCB	MARTIN	2	1	3	3	2	2	2	1	1	1	
WCNC	6 NEWS AT 6PM	2	3	1	1	1	1	2	2	4	3	5
WFVT	FRESH PRINCE	1	1	2	2	2	1	1	1	1		1
WJZY	GRACE-FIRE MF	3	2	2	3	4	3	3	3	2	2	1
WNSC	NEWSHOUR-LEHR											
WSOC	EYEWIT NWS 6	11	13	5	6	7	8	9	11	17	14	23
WTVI	VARIOUS											
WUNG	NEWSHOUR-LEHR											
	HUT/PUT/TOTALS*	34	37	22	26	26	28	29	31	42	38	52
6:30PM												
WAXN	JUDGE JUDY	2	2	2	2	2	2	2	2	2	2	2
WBTV	CBS EVE NWS	6	8	1	3	4	5	5	6	10	7	13
WCCB	SIMPSONS	3	2	5	5	4	3	3	2	1	1	1
WCNC	NBC NITELY NWS	2	3	1	1	1	1	2	2	4	2	6
WFVT	HANGN-MR COOPR	2	1	3	3	2	2	2	1	1	1	1
WJZY	GRACE-FRE MF B	3	3	2	4	4	4	4	4	2	3	1
WNSC	NEWSHOUR-LEHR											
WSOC	ABC WORLD NWS	9	11	3	4	5	6	7	8	14	12	19
WTVI	VARIOUS											
WUNG	NEWSHOUR-LEHR											
	HUT/PUT/TOTALS*	35	37	26	29	29	30	31	32	40	38	49
7:00PM												
WAXN	JUDGE JUDY B	2	2	1	2	2	2	2	3	3	3	3
WBTV	ACCESS HOLLYWD	4	5	1	2	3	3	3	4	6	4	6
WCCB	HOME IMPR MF B	4	4	4	5	5	5	5	5	3	4	3
WCNC	JEOPARDY	5	6	2	2	3	3	3	4	8	5	13
WFVT	LIVING SINGLE	2	2	4	4	4	2	2	2	1	1	1
WJZY	SEINFELD	4	4	3	6	6	5	6	5	3	4	2
WNSC	NITE BSNSS RPT											
WSOC	INSIDE EDITION	6	7	2	2	3	4	4	5	9	8	13
WTVI	NEWSHOUR-LEHR											1
WUNG	NITE BSNSS RPT											
	HUT/PUT/TOTALS*	40	43	26	32	34	35	36	38	47	41	57
7:30PM												
WAXN	AVG ALL WKS	2	2		1	1	2	2	3	2	3	2
	#REAL-HWY PATRL	2	2	1	1	1	2	1	2	3	3	3
	REAL-HWY PATRL	2	2		1	1	2	2	3	2	2	2
WBTV	EXTRA	4	5	1	2	3	3	4	4	6	5	7
WCCB	HOME IMPROV MF	5	5	5	5	5	5	5	5	4	5	4
WCNC	WHEEL-FORTNE	6	8	2	3	4	3	3	4	10	6	16
WFVT	AVG. ALL WKS	3	2	4	4	4	3	3	2	1	2	1
	#FRESH PRINCE	2	1	5	3	2	2	1	1	1	2	1
	FRESH PRINCE	3	2	4	4	5	3	3	3	1	1	1
WJZY	AVG. ALL WKS	3	4	2	4	5	5	5	5	3	4	3
	#FRASIER	3	4	2	4	4	4	5	5	3	4	2
	FRASIER	4	4	2	5	5	5	5	5	3	4	3
WNSC	VARIOUS											
WSOC	ENT TONIGHT 30	6	7	4	4	4	5	5	6	9	8	12
WTVI	NEWSHOUR-LEHR											
WUNG	NC NOW											
	HUT/PUT/TOTALS*	43	46	27	35	37	38	40	42	50	44	59

STATION	PROGRAM	WOMEN 18+	12-24	18-34	18-49	25-49	25-54	WKG	MEN 18+	18-34	18-49	21-49	25-49	25-54	TNS 12-17	CHILD 2-11	6-11
	R.S.E. THRESHOLDS 25+% (1 S.E.) 4 WK AVG 50+%	1 LT	5 1	3 1	1 LT	1 LT	1 LT	1 LT	1 LT	5 1	2 LT	2 LT	2 LT	1 LT	7 1	4 1	6 1
6:00PM																	
WAXN	REAL-HWY PATRL	1					1		1	1	1	1	1	1			
WBTV	WBTV NWS-600P	9	1	4	6	7	7	7	8	4	6	6	7	7	1	2	1
WCCB	MARTIN	1	3	2	2	2	2	2	1	2	1	1	1	1	4	2	2
WCNC	6 NEWS AT 6PM	3			1	2	2	2	3	2	2	2	2	2			
WFVT	FRESH PRINCE	1	3	3	1	1	1	1		1					2	3	4
WJZY	GRACE-FIRE MF	3	3	5	4	5	4	4	2	2	2	2	2	2	2	4	5
WNSC	NEWSHOUR-LEHR																
WSOC	EYEWIT NWS 6	15	4	8	10	11	13	13	12	6	7	7	8	8	4	2	2
WTVI	VARIOUS																
WUNG	NEWSHOUR-LEHR																
	HUT/PUT/TOTALS*	40	24	28	31	33	35	35	33	24	26	27	27	28	23	27	31
6:30PM																	
WAXN	JUDGE JUDY	2	1	2	2	2	2	2	2	2	2	1	1	1			
WBTV	CBS EVE NWS	8	1	4	5	6	5	7	7	4	5	5	6	6	1	2	1
WCCB	SIMPSONS	2	4	4	2	2	2	2	2	5	3	3	3	3	6	3	2
WCNC	NBC NITELY NWS	3		1	1	2	2	3	3	1	1	2	2	2			
WFVT	HANGN-MR COOPR	2	5	4	2	2	2	2	1	1	1	1	1	1	3	3	4
WJZY	GRACE-FRE MF B	4	2	6	5	6	6	4	2	2	2	2	2	2	3	4	6
WNSC	NEWSHOUR-LEHR																
WSOC	ABC WORLD NWS	12	3	5	7	8	10	11	10	4	6	6	6	7	3	3	3
WTVI	VARIOUS																
WUNG	NEWSHOUR-LEHR																
	HUT/PUT/TOTALS*	39	27	30	32	34	35	36	34	28	28	28	29	30	29	28	30
7:00PM																	
WAXN	JUDGE JUDY B	3	1	2	2	2	2	2	2	2	2	2	2	3	1	1	1
WBTV	ACCESS HOLLYWD	5		3	4	4	4	5	5	2	3	3	3	3	1	2	2
WCCB	HOME IMPR MF B	3	3	3	4	4	4	4	5	7	5	5	6	5	4	6	6
WCNC	JEOPARDY	7	2	3	3	4	4	5	5	2	2	2	2	3	1	1	1
WFVT	LIVING SINGLE	2	7	5	3	2	2	3	1	2	2	2	2	2	4	3	4
WJZY	SEINFELD	4	2	6	5	6	6	5	5	7	6	6	6	5	3	2	3
WNSC	NITE BSNSS RPT																
WSOC	INSIDE EDITION	8	2	3	5	5	7	7	6	2	4	3	4	4	1	2	2
WTVI	NEWSHOUR-LEHR																
WUNG	NITE BSNSS RPT																
	HUT/PUT/TOTALS*	45	26	34	35	38	39	41	40	33	34	35	36	37	27	35	38
7:30PM																	
WAXN	AVG ALL WKS	1		1	1	1	2	1	3	2	3	3	3	4		2	2
	#REAL-HWY PATRL	1		1	1	2	1	1	3	2	2	2	2	3			
	REAL-HWY PATRL	1		1	1	1	2	1	2	2	3	3	4	4		2	3
WBTV	EXTRA	5	1	3	4	5	5	5	4	2	3	3	3	3	1	3	2
WCCB	HOME IMPROV MF	4	3	4	4	5	5	5	5	7	6	6	6	6	6	5	6
WCNC	WHEEL-FORTNE	9	3	5	4	4	6	6	6	3	3	3	2	3	2	2	2
WFVT	AVG. ALL WKS	3	7	5	3	3	2	3	2	3	2	2	2	2	4	3	5
	#FRESH PRINCE	1	9	3	2	1	1	3	1	1	2	2	2	2	7	3	
	FRESH PRINCE	3	7	6	4	3	3	4	2	4	2	3	2	2	4	4	5
WJZY	AVG. ALL WKS	4	1	5	5	5	5	5	4	4	4	5	5	4	2	2	3
	#FRASIER	3	1	4	4	5	5	4	4	5	5	5	6	5	2	2	2
	FRASIER	5	2	7	6	6	6	7	3	4	4	4	4	4	3	2	4
WNSC	VARIOUS																
WSOC	ENT TONIGHT 30	9	3	5	6	7	8	8	6	3	4	4	4	4	3	2	2
WTVI	NEWSHOUR-LEHR																
WUNG	NC NOW																
	HUT/PUT/TOTALS*	49	30	39	40	43	44	46	42	35	37	38	40	41	29	40	44

FIGURE B-2 A typical page from a diary-driven ratings book. Courtesy Nielsen Media Research.

message over a given time period. This is also called the cumulative or unduplicated audience. Even if homes or people are exposed more than once, they're only counted once. Therefore, the maximum reach is 100 percent of the universe. (This is not to be confused with achieving a 100 GRP [gross rating points] schedule.)

So if reach is the number of different people, frequency is the average number of times your audience is exposed to your message.

A good rule of thumb is to make sure that your frequency is three or more, but no more than nine. After nine, you're wasting your resources. To get a reach and frequency report, you'll need to order special reports or have access to software. This is where you'll get to know your station research director or the sales department's designated research maven.

Another term you may run into is gross rating points or GRPs, or simply "Grips." Grips are the sum of all rating points achieved in a given schedule. If you want to achieve a 100 GRP schedule for a week against a given program, simply add up the total audience rating points for each time you plan to air a spot for that program. Note that a 100 GRP schedule does not mean you have reached 100 percent of your audience.

```
PAGE 2

CHARLOTTE                                                              WEEKDAY OVERNIGHT REPORT
Source: NSI      379 reporting households
Daily Grid

 TIME  HUT  3 WBTV C    RTG SHR  9 WSOC A      RTG SHR  36 WCNC N       RTG SHR  18 WCCB F       RTG SHR  46 WJZY I
 5:00p  44  WBTV NWS-500P 8.4 19  EYEWIT NWS 5  11.1 25  6 NEWS AT 5PM   2.9  7   JUDGE JUDY      3.7  8   STEP BY STEP
        47   8.4 18  46  8.4 18   11.9 26  46  12.7 27   2.9  6  46  2.9 6  4.0  9  46  4.2 9   2.0  4  46
 5:30p  47  WBTV NWS-530P 10.3 22 EYEWIT NWS 530 11.9 25  6 NEWS AT 530P  3.2  7   JUDGE JUDY B    4.2  9   FULL HOUSE
        51  10.2 21  49 10.0 20   12.3 25  49  12.7 25   3.3  7  49  3.4 7  4.2  9  49  4.2 8   3.0  6  49
 6:00p  52  WBTV NWS-600P 11.9 23 EYEWIT NWS 6  14.5 28  6 NEWS AT 6PM   3.7  7   HOME IMPROV MF  4.2  8   ROSEANNE
        50  10.0 20   14.2 28  51 14.0 28   4.0  8  51  4.2 8   3.8 7  51  3.4 7  1.6  3  51
 6:30p  49   7.7 16  ABC-WORLD NWS 10.8 22   NBC NITELY NWS 4.5  9   GRACE-FIRE MF B
        50   9.2 18  50  7.4 15    9.6 19  50  8.4 17   4.9 10  50  5.3 10  4.4 9  50  4.2 8   2.6  5  50
 7:00p  50  CBS EVE NWS  7.4 15   INSIDE EDITION 5.5 11  JEOPARDY        8.2 16   FRIENDS         4.7  9   GRACE-FIRE MF
        50   6.9 14  50  6.3 13    5.3 11  50  5.0 10   8.7 17  50  9.2 19  4.9 10 50  5.0 10  2.1  4  50
 7:30p  48  NANNY        5.0 10   ENT TONIGHT 30 6.1 13  WHEEL-FORTNE    8.7 18   FRIENDS B       4.2  9   SEINFELD
        50   5.0 10  49  5.0 10    5.9 12  49  5.8 12   8.6 18  49  8.4 17  4.6 9  49  5.0 10  4.2  9  49
 8:00p  50  JAG-CBS      7.9 16   HOME IMPRV-ABC 7.4 15  3-ROCK-SUN-NBC  5.3 10   FOX STNLY-FNL1  1.8  4   MOESHA-UPN
        51   6.9 13    8.0 16  51  8.7 17   4.4  9  51  3.4 7  (SABRE&STARS) 0.5 1  4.1  8  51
 8:30p  53   7.9 15  HUGHLEYS-ABC  8.4 16   NEWSRADIO-NBC  3.7  7   0.5  1   CLUELESS-UPN
        57   8.0 15  53  9.2 16    8.2 15  55  7.9 14   4.2  8  55  4.7 8   1.6 3   3.2  6  55
 9:00p  61  CBS TUE MOV  10.3 17  SPIN CITY-ABC 7.9 13  JUST SHOOT-NBC  5.0 10   MARTIN          1.1  2   MALCOLMED-UPN
        62  (EVERYNG-GAIN) 10.0 16  7.9 13  61  7.9 13   4.6  8  61  4.2 7   0.5 1   4.0  6  61
 9:30p  64  10.6 17  SPORTS NTE-ABC 6.9 11   3-ROCK-SP-NBC  4.2  7   0.5  1   BETWN BROS-UPN
        63   8.7 14    6.1 10  63  5.3  8   4.0  6  63  3.7 6   1.1 2   5.3  8  63
10:00p  59   8.2 14  NYPD BLUE-ABC 5.0  8   DATELNE NBC-TU 5.8 10   2.4  4   FRASIER
        59   9.5 16    4.2  7   5.5  9   2.4 4   3.8  6  59
10:30p  56   9.0 16    5.3  9   5.5  9   1.3 2   MAD ABOUT YOU
        53   9.5 16  60  9.5 18    5.1  9  57  6.1 11   5.4 10  57  5.0 9   1.3 2  57  1.8 3   3.0  6  55
11:00p  50  WBTV NWS AT 11 8.4 17 EYEWIT NWS 11 10.3 21  6NWS NIGHTCAST 5.0 10   MARTIN          1.8  4   MARRIED-CHLDRN
        46   7.3 15  48  6.1 13   10.9 23  48  11.6 25   4.4  9  48  3.7 8   1.8 4  48  1.8 4   3.2  7  48
11:30p  42  D LETTRMAN-CBS 4.7 11 ABC-NITELINE  8.7 21  TONITE SHW-NBC  4.0  9   SIMPSONS        1.8  4   NEWSRADIO
        36   3.2  9    7.4 19  39  6.1 17   3.7 10   1.6 4  39  1.3 4   2.5  6  39
12:00m  32   2.6  8  POLIT INCT-ABC 5.0 16   3.7 12  JRRY SPRINGR R  2.9  9   NEWSRADIO B
        28   3.0  9  34  1.6  6    4.4 15  30  3.7 13   3.5 10  34  2.6 9   2.4 8   2.4  8  30
12:30a  23  C KILBORN-CBS 0.5  2   MILLS LANE    3.4 15  C O'BRIEN-NBC  1.8  8   2.4 10   CHEERS
        22   1.3  6    2.8 12  23  2.1 10   1.8  8   2.4 9  26  2.1 10  1.1  5  23
 1:00a  21   1.1  5  INSIDE EDITION 1.6  8   1.6  8  RICKI LAKE      1.6  8   CHEERS B
        19   0.9  4  21  0.8  4    1.5  7  20  1.3  7   1.6  7  21  1.1 5   1.8 10  1.1  5  20
 1:30a  18  HARD COPY    0.8  4   VIEW-ABC      1.3  7  LATER-NBC       1.1  6   1.3  7   NEWLYWED GAME
```

FIGURE B-3   A typical overnight rating sheet. Courtesy Nielsen Media Research.

The Nielsen rating book contains a snapshot of your market's viewing patterns for the 4 weeks it covers. You will note significant viewing pattern changes among the November book, the May book, and the July book. This is usually owing to seasonal lifestyle changes. But, you want to know, or your boss wants to know, how many people does a rating point represent?

Here's where you pull out the calculator, ruler, and the magnifying glass.

First, find the listing of the television households, which is usually on the first or second page of the book. In a given market, Nielsen estimated there were 978,100 households. Dividing that by the universe of 100 percent gives you one rating point equals 9,781 households. If you're able to show a two-rating point increase, your station will have gained a potential of 19,562 households! And those are numbers your sales department should be able to merchandise to clients for increased sales!

So far, we've discussed the rating book. Many television markets are also metered. The metering process provides stations and advertisers with a way to check on how well they're doing on an overnight time frame as the programs relate to households (not individual demographics). Rather than having someone in the household fill a diary with viewing information, the Nielsen company monitors every television tuner in a sample household. This includes the main television, televisions in the kitchen or bedrooms, the tuners in VCRs, and even a tuner in a personal computer video card, if one is in the household.

The good news is that these overnights, as they're called, provide instant feedback on what a station—or a station's competition—is doing. The bad news is they don't provide demographic information. You, and your sales department, have no way of knowing if your 25 rating is made up of highly desirable adults 18 to 49 years of age or if you have somehow cornered the market in Latvian penguins.

The Nielsen rating system is the main way television stations gather audience research information, but not the only way. Other ways of gathering information include telephone surveys; face-to-face surveys, usually conducted in shopping malls; mail surveys, which can also be an effective way of driving viewing in addition to gathering information; newly emerging e-mail surveys; and focus groups.

This has been a basic look at the sometimes baffling world of ratings. Ratings are the key to understanding the effective use of on-air promotion and planning campaigns. Take some time to go over a rating book and see what else you can learn about your station and your competitors. Turn the ratings from unfamiliar territory to a useful tool.

Subject Index

Page numbers followed by "t" indicate a table; page numbers followed by "f" indicate a figure.